W9-CQH-114

GUIDEPOSTS

Angels Ever Near

EVERYWHERE FROM A TO Z

Angels Ever Near

EVERYWHERE FROM A TO Z

Compiled and edited by Evelyn Bence

CARMEL, NEW YORK 10512

www.guidepostsbooks.com

Copyright © 2001 by Guideposts, Carmel, New York 10512. All rights reserved.

No part of this publication may be reproduced, stored in a retrieval system or transmitted in any form or by any means, electronic, mechanical, photocopying, recording or otherwise without the written permission of the publisher. Inquiries should be addressed to the Rights & Permissions Department, Guideposts, 16 E. 34th St., New York, NY 10016.

Every attempt has been made to credit the sources of copyrighted material used in this book. If any such acknowledgment has been inadvertently omitted or miscredited, receipt of such information would be appreciated.

ACKNOWLEDGMENTS

All material that originally appeared in *Angels on Earth* is reprinted with permission. Copyright © 1995, 1996, 1997, 1998, 1999 and 2000 by Guideposts, Carmel, New York 10512. All rights reserved.

All Scripture quotations, unless otherwise noted, are taken from *The Holy Bible, New International Version.* Copyright © 1973, 1978, 1984 International Bible Society. Used by permission of Zondervan Bible Publishers.

Scripture quotations marked (KJV) are taken from *The King James Version.*

Evelyn Bence's photograph is © WG Dusterwald, www.dustyphoto.com.

www.guidepostsbooks.com
Guideposts Book and Inspirational Media Division
Edited by Evelyn Bence
Designed by Patty Tyler
Jacket and interior illustrations by Edgar Jerins
Typeset by Allentown Digital Services Division
of R.R. Donnelley & Sons
Printed in the United States of America

TABLE OF CONTENTS

TABLE OF CONTENTS

NTRODUCTION

But I trust in you, O Lord;
I say, "You are my God."
My times are in your hands. . . .
                    ~Psalm 31:14–15

If you make the Most High your dwelling. . .
he will command his angels concerning you
to guard you in all your ways.
                    ~Psalm 91:9, 11

ll your ways." That means no mountain is high enough . . . no storm fierce enough . . . to keep God's angels from finding us.

This is dramatically clear from the first to the last page of these compelling, true stories that mark God's merciful care—everywhere from A to Z.

Every book takes shape in a unique way. For *Angels Ever Near,* we started with a title and a collection of great angel stories that spanned the globe and most of the twentieth century. We looked at the wealth of material in front of us, selected from *Angels on Earth* magazine, and asked, "How can we best organize these stories so the message is clear—that God's messengers can guide us, protect us, strengthen us anywhere?" We knew a metaphor might work, but only if it was grounded in a timeless spiritual reality.

That's when a descriptive Bible verse came to mind that il-lustrates the greatness of God. In Revelation 1:8 God says He is "the Alpha and the Omega," the A and Z of the Greek alphabet. And where does that all-encompassing God meet us? Everywhere. In set-tings from A to Z that stretch from the A to the Z of life. In that always-and-everywhere realm, God is personally involved in our daily lives, directing His representatives, His angels, to give us courage to do His will.

We know that some readers will sit down and enjoy this book

because their own lives have been changed by the sight or sound or touch of an angel. Maybe you, like the men and women who tell their stories in these pages, know that after such an encounter life is never again the same. You stand amazed at the wonder of God's love.

Other readers will read these pages with a different kind of wonder: *Why haven't I seen an angel's wing or heard a heavenly song?* No human can answer that question. Isaiah 55:9 says that God's ways are not our ways. But we notice one theme that keeps coming up in these stories: God and His angels are near even when their presence is not miraculously evident. Consider these examples:

- The man who identified himself as Evelyn Fehlberg's guardian angel walked into a crowd, out of her sight. "But," she notes in "Subway Sentinel," "the One Who sent him would forever be by my side."
- In "Mystery of the Missing Report Card," Pamela Keyser describes only one angelic visit, one dark, scary night of her childhood. But she knows that's just a piece of the bigger life story. "I was on my own from a very early age, but I was never, ever alone."
- Reflecting on the sight of three otherworldly beings at her bedside, in "A Familiar Light" Robin Langston Beiermeister writes, "I know these angels. They have been with me all my life."

Even if you've never seen or heard their presence, know that God and God's angels are near. In faith, take a leap and claim the Psalms as your own: All your times are in God's hands. All your ways are guarded. Every day remind yourself that no mountain is high enough . . . no storm fierce enough . . . to keep God's angels from finding anyone, even you.

~Evelyn Bence

Angels Ever Near

EVERYWHERE FROM A TO Z

IR

Psalm 139:8 says that God is present, even if we "go up to the heavens." Flight attendant June Bussard and pilot Craig Silver are sure of it. Experienced fliers, they could tell something was very wrong in the cockpit. They knew the good earth was a long way down, and yet they sensed a clear guiding hand that averted disaster in the air.

Flight Attendant

by June E. Bussard

hurried across the tarmac at the Kansas City airport and up the stairwell into the DC-4. The service trucks were already pulling away from the plane as I set about doing last-minute preparations for our flight to Burbank, California. I loved my work as a stewardess with Great Lakes Airlines, but being awakened in the middle of the night was one of the drawbacks. "Sorry, June," Capt. Jack Pedesky had said when he called. "The scheduled girl sprained her ankle." We were still called girls in those days.

Walking through the empty plane at midnight, I went over my checklist: blankets, pillows, the items we graciously referred to as burp cups, and in the tiny galley, sandwiches, snacks and coffee. *I'll need some of that coffee myself,* I decided, unable to stifle a yawn.

My last chore was to slip freshly laundered covers over the headrests of all seventy-five seats. With a sigh I finished a row and glanced down the aisle. Near the tail section, I was startled to see another stewardess smoothing the headrest covers. She wore our airline's light blue uniform, her dark hair pulled back in a bun, her cap slightly tilted. She seemed vaguely familiar, but what was she doing here? Only one stewardess was ever assigned to these flights.

I blinked and looked again. The aisle was empty. *Am I so exhausted I'm seeing things?*

I rubbed my eyes. The girl's face popped into my mind, and I suddenly remembered where I'd seen her—in a dream just the other night. It was the same girl, hair pulled back, cap tilted. In my dream she'd stood at the door of a plane, welcoming me. *What could it mean?*

Hearing familiar voices in the stairwell, I straightened my uniform and managed a smile. Captain Jack and Capt. Frank MacDonald, the copilot, entered the plane. "Cabin checklist complete," I said. "Thanks, June," said Captain Jack, handing me a flight manifest. "Really sorry about calling you at this hour."

"That's all right, sir," I said. "It's my job."

"A storm front's moving across," he informed me. "We'll have rough weather till we get above it."

Captain MacDonald squeezed my shoulder. We'd flown together many times. "Good to see you, June," he said. "How about breakfast at Bubba's when we land? My treat."

"Sure thing, Mac," I responded with a grin.

Our full passenger list included two women with children and many servicemen bound for Korea. Everyone boarded and got settled in a seat.

Soon after takeoff we hit the storm. The plane surged in up- and downdrafts. Jagged lightning tore the sky, bathing the cabin with an eerie glow. Almost every passenger was afraid, and some were sick. A stewardess is instructed to stay buckled in her jump seat during turbulence, but the passengers needed my attention. I tightroped my way through the aisle, gripping the seats for balance, calming nerves, handing out pillows. Glancing up I noticed sparks coming from the number three inboard engine. It wasn't unusual. Sometimes the exhaust threw off a trail of sparks.

"Please stay in your seats," I said, trying to seem calm. Suddenly more sparks caught my eye through the rain-drenched windows. Prickles ran up my neck, and I made my way to the cockpit and opened the door. I told Captain Jack about the sparking. "Good eye," he said. He began a check of the instruments as I went back into the cabin.

Lightning flashes bounced blue darts of light through the cabin. I braced myself, my hip against a seat, waiting for the next downdraft. I watched the inboard engine through the windows. Everything seemed normal, so why did I feel a current of fear, almost like the lightning itself, coursing through my body?

I'm just tired, I told myself, and went back to soothing my passengers. As I struggled along the aisle, I heard a strange whooshing sound. Then a long silence, and abruptly a brilliant sheet of flame shot from the number three engine.

"Fire! Fire!" a woman screamed. The flame snapped and fluttered along the fuselage like a monstrous flag. No, no, no! The roar of the fire could be heard through the thick glass portholes and riveted steel. Everyone panicked. The passengers closest to the number three engine clawed their way out of their seats, trying to get to the other side of the plane.

I grabbed the intercom. "Return to your seats!" I shouted. "Do not leave your seats!"

A woman stumbled into the aisle, and I turned to a serviceman near me. "Soldier," I shouted, "help that lady back to her seat!" Seeing stripes on another serviceman's sleeve, I said, "Sergeant, assist the passengers!" I shouted over and over, "There is no place to go! You are safe only in your seats! Tighten your seat belts!"

I kept calling out instructions until there was a semblance of order. Lurching through the cockpit door, I froze. Alarm lights flashed crazily. Every instrument on the panel had gone haywire. The pilots struggled with their controls and rudders, hands frantically reaching for switches. I clung to the doorframe, terrified.

Then I saw her.

Standing between the pilots was the stewardess from my dream. She placed a hand on each pilot's shoulder and then vanished.

My breath caught in my throat, but I heard Captain Jack's confident voice speaking into his radio: "Fire out of control in three. Forced landing. Strip at Gage, Oklahoma. Estimate, twenty minutes."

I knew what had to be done. I made my way through the cabin,

dodging objects spilling out of the overhead storage bins. The women began to wail. "It will be all right," I said to the passengers as I rushed by. *Dear Lord, help me. I can't fail these people.* Reaching my jump seat, I buckled in, my body aching from the pounding. Then the pilot's voice rang out over the intercom: "Touchdown in eight minutes. Obey every instruction from your stewardess."

The galley bulkhead shuddered against my back, and I tightened the belt across my hips. I felt afraid and terribly alone, but I knew my duty. Lives depended on me. I pressed my intercom, raising my voice over the roaring flames. "When I give the order, pillow on lap, face in pillow, grasp ankles. Do not move from that position until we come to a complete stop."

The plane started to descend. I explained into the mike, "We're in a landing pattern. Captain Pedesky is slipping the plane sideways, away from the flames. He flew bombers over Germany. He will land this plane safely."

Then the power failed. No mike, no lights. Nothing but a roaring inferno out there in the night! I prayed for the children, the women, the young soldiers, the pilots—everyone aboard the plane. Would the landing strip be long enough for this big DC-4?

Downdrafts caught the ship. I saw a woman's arm drop and drag the floor. She'd fainted. How many others? *Please, Lord, be merciful.* The clunk of the wheels being lowered startled me. The pilot was pulling back power. Gear down, flaps down. I shouted, "Bend over. Grab your ankles. Bend over. Pass it on. We're going to land. Pass it on. Bend over. Grab your ankles. Stay that way!"

I hugged my knees. I heard the sound of a wheel screeching on solid ground, then the wheel screeching again.

Dear God, we're down!

I ripped the seat belt off and staggered toward an exit hatch. The right wing was in flames. With a loud crash, the plane lurched over onto the flaming wing. We spun around like a giant top, and I was flung down the aisle until my body landed with a crushing crack on my head. Blackness, then bright-colored points of light. Roaring, then peacefulness washing over me. Above me suddenly was the smiling face of my dream stewardess. I strained to reach up to her, but soft words came: "No, June. It is not time."

Strong hands lifted me. Cries and shouts filled the air. I marshaled all my strength and rushed to the hatch, grasping the handle. "Help me!" I shouted to a sergeant. "Pull back, then push up. Try again. Pull back again hard. Twist. Now up. Again!" Together we pressed and finally the door unlatched. A blast of cool air swept over us.

There was no panic. The passengers stood up quickly, not speaking, just hurrying. "Here, these snaps release the slide," I said. "There, you two jump down. Hold the slide securely."

As the soldiers helped people out of the plane, I squeezed past passengers in the aisle. "Keep moving!" I shouted. "We'll all be out soon." I helped a soldier carry the woman who had fainted.

Mac grabbed my arm. "Jump, June. They're all out. Go!" He pushed me down the slide. Captain Jack was there, helping me up, and we hurried after the passengers to a small incline a short distance away. Just as we got there, a huge explosion threw us to the ground. The plane had blown up. I felt the cool earth, wet, solid and secure beneath me. Another blast and the ground trembled. "Thank You, dear Lord," I gasped. "We are all safe!"

Immediately my mind saw the face of the young stewardess. The Lord's angel had been with us on the flight!

Go East, Young Man

by Craig Silver

The flight wasn't supposed to present any particular challenge that June day. All I had to do was pilot my boss, Bob, in a single-engine, red and white Cessna 210 from Syracuse, New York, to Leesburg, Virginia. Two hours, two hundred sixty nautical miles. No big deal.

"We'll be home for supper," I said to Bob. My only concern was a series of thunderstorms along the Appalachians.

I'd filed a flight plan that noted the Cessna wasn't equipped with radar or lightning detection equipment. I'd be depending on some sharp air-traffic controllers to keep me out of trouble, but that's what ATC was for.

After ground check, Bob and I put on our headsets to talk over the engine noise, and we launched into the afternoon drizzle. ATC directed me around a thunderstorm cell and got us back on course at an altitude of nine thousand feet. As we cruised on automatic pilot, virtually every electrical device on the plane was helping guide the way. Red, yellow and green lights lit up the instrument panel, making it look like a Christmas tree.

But suddenly it was as if someone pulled the plug. All the lights went dark. The automatic pilot lost its electronic inputs. The plane went into a dive and plummeted toward the ground.

"Bob, we're in trouble!" I shouted as I pulled back on the steering column with all my might with one hand while switching off the autopilot with the other. I had to shout because our headsets were out, too.

"Yeah, I know," he called back, holding on for dear life as I managed to bring up the nose of the plane.

I checked the circuit breakers. None of them had popped, so there'd be no easy fix. Not one electrical device was working! Without radios we couldn't get help from the air-traffic controllers. Without my transponder they wouldn't even see me on radar. But I had one ace up my sleeve, my trusty portable radio.

I handed it to Bob. "Punch in these numbers," I said, giving him the emergency frequency. He was having a hard time hearing me over the roar of the engine. I repeated the numbers and plugged my headset into the portable. "Mayday-Mayday-Mayday, this is November five four five one Victor, over." No response. "Mayday-Mayday-Mayday, this is November five four five one Victor, over." Nothing. I said it again. Still nothing. "It's no use, Bob. The batteries must be low."

All at once a hole opened in the clouds. I could see the mountains below. I descended and leveled out only three hundred feet above the rugged terrain. "I think it'll work out," I said to Bob without conviction. He gave me a look that seemed to say I would never see another raise.

My intent was to continue south-by-southeast, because I knew there were mountains to the west and I wasn't familiar with what was to the east. I thought I was heading south. I checked the gyro compass. It read "East." I tried to turn south but the plane wouldn't bank. I felt resistance in the wheel, as if a weight were pushing on it. Or maybe an angel was sitting on the left wing fighting my every attempt to bank to the right. This plane was going east, and that's all there was to it.

Finally, I submitted. Wanting to seem like I had things under control, I told Bob, "I think we'll head east for a while. If you see an airport, let me know."

Seconds later he pointed out the window and shouted, "There's an airport right there."

Sure enough, through the rain and fog and mist I could just make out a short landing strip surrounded by mountains. Could I land on it without the electrical wing flaps that would normally slow me down? I had to try.

"Whatever you do, Bob, don't lose sight of that airport," I called out.

I circled around to line up my approach. Anxious, I went in too fast. The wheels touched down, but there wasn't enough room to

stop. I pulled up ten degrees on the stick, pushed in the throttle, took off again. I circled, lined up, slowed the Cessna to just above stall speed and managed to touch down and stop with room to spare.

Taxiing up to the field's one small building, Bob and I looked at each other. "Praise the Lord," we exclaimed in unison.

The next day I tried to figure out the silent nudge to "go east." The chart showed only that one small airport in the region, and it was situated due east from the point where the electricity went out on my aircraft. When all else failed, God Himself had guided me in the right direction.

Angels from the realms of glory,
Wing your flight o'er all the earth.

~ James Montgomery

EDSIDE

"Through the long night watches, may God's angels spread
Their white wings about me, watching 'round my bed."

A hundred years ago Rev. Sabine Baring-Gould penned these lines as
a good-night prayer for the children in his church-school. What an
appropriate and powerful request, even for grown ups. In response to
desperate night-time prayers, Robin Langston Beiermeister and Delilah
LaViano saw the angels watching at their bedside. Even if you don't see
them, they're there!

A Familiar Light

by Robin Langston Beiermeister

I tossed several shopping bags full of Christmas gifts into the backseat of my car and joined the stream of traffic fighting to get out of the mall parking lot. I was running late for my annual appointment with my gynecologist, which I had already put off for some time. Even without the seasonal hustle-bustle, I was busy looking after four daughters with my husband, Geoffrey. Besides, it didn't seem too pressing; I was thirty-seven and in good health. At the doctor's office I waited impatiently for the exam to be over with so I could go home and read Christmas stories to my "babies," two-year-old Hayley and four-year-old Ryan.

A few days later I got a phone call. The doctor said my Pap smear result was slightly abnormal and I should be tested again in a few months. *Just some mistake at the lab,* I thought. I felt fine and was so busy planning our holiday activities I didn't have time to worry. But three months later, when the second test also came back abnormal, my doctor scheduled a biopsy.

The day before the procedure I took a long walk, trying to calm my fears. As I turned a corner I came to a little gift shop. My eye was drawn to a beautiful gold cross in the window, gleaming in the rays of the late afternoon sun. I felt compelled to go in and buy it. Outside again, I clasped it around my neck and felt less afraid.

When the biopsy results were ready, a nurse called to set up an immediate appointment to come in and talk to the doctor. "Try not to worry," she said, but worry was all I could do. The next day, as I sat in the doctor's quiet office waiting for him to explain the test results, I kept reaching for the gold cross around my neck. He said the biopsy revealed well-defined cancer cells. I gripped the edge of his huge oak desk with both hands and closed my eyes. For the past seven months it had been just a nagging question mark on my medical chart. Now I had to accept the fact that I had a potentially deadly disease.

"We could schedule a full hysterectomy right now. Or we could do another procedure to find out more about what we're facing," the doctor said.

I shook my head and met his gaze. I didn't want to deal with uncertainty anymore. I just wanted things to get back to the way they were.

"No, I want the operation," I said.

He nodded. "It will be impossible to tell until the surgery how far-reaching the cancer is. But we'll have a specialist standing by in case it's spread beyond the cervix."

I went through the rest of the day with worries and regrets turning in my mind. Why had I put off the Pap smear for so long? What if the cancer had already spread?

That night I sat wearily on the edge of Ryan's bed as she finished saying her prayers.

"And please, God, take away the bad stuff that's making Mommy sick, so she can be happy again."

I pulled her close, my throat tightening, then tucked her in quickly. I could not break down in front of my children. *Lord, give me the strength to endure this struggle.*

The night before my surgery I checked into the hospital for pre-op procedures. I wasn't allowed to eat anything. I had a bit of a sore throat, so I was given antibiotics through an IV line. I lay staring at the ceiling, just wanting the cancer out of me. I felt as though there were a huge clock ticking above my head, counting down the minutes till the disease would take over my whole body. I was racing against that clock.

By morning my sore throat had become a full-fledged fever. My doctor couldn't operate. He sent me home and rescheduled the surgery for ten days later. The fever persisted. When the new date arrived my temperature was 104 degrees.

"Why is this happening? Can't you give me something?" I pleaded with my doctor on the phone.

"Robin, the tests show what you have isn't bacterial, so antibiotics aren't effective. The only thing I can tell you to do right now is wait the virus out. Stress and worry will only make it worse. Try to rest."

Easier said than done. Unable to look after my youngest children, I felt totally helpless. Geoffrey and my older girls took over their care and made sure there were always fluids and Tylenol by my bedside. My arms ached to hold my little ones, but I was so sick and weak I could hardly lift a water glass.

That night I lay in bed alone; Geoffrey had been sleeping downstairs because of my fever. I tossed and turned. How could I fight the cancer when this fever was making surgery impossible? What if it were already too late? Would my girls have to grow up without me?

I wrapped myself in the large violet and yellow quilt, my grandmother's favorite. I felt a sharp tug and looked down. My cross was caught in the threads of the quilt. I disentangled it and ran a finger over its surface. Then, squeezing it tightly in my palm, I prayed. *God, please take away this fever so I can have the operation.* I had always had faith, but I had never prayed like that. Over and over, waking myself out of a fitful slumber, I begged God to make me well enough to have the surgery. I prayed without pride and without doubt. It felt as though I had reached the very core of my soul and my prayer was coming from there. Even as I continued to shiver, then sweat, in the throes of fever, I asked Him to send me help.

In the early hours of morning I awoke after a short doze. But I couldn't open my eyes and my body felt strange, as if it were gently vibrating. When I finally managed to raise my eyelids, I looked down and saw through the patchwork quilt; I saw my body bathed in a

golden-green light that outlined my shape. My eyes followed the light to its source. Three beings who appeared to be composed of pure light were at the foot of the bed. A dazzling brightness spread out behind them like wings, and the beams that encircled me seemed to emanate from their hands. Now I was fully awake, fully aware.

For a moment I was terrified. Then I understood clearly the message: "You are safe. You are loved. Go back to sleep." I obeyed. But soon the enormity of what I was experiencing crept back into my mind. I opened my eyes to see what the beings were doing.

My body was still enveloped in light. I didn't dare move. The angel on the right tilted her head toward the one in the center as if to communicate something. *I know these angels,* I thought suddenly. *They have been with me before. They are here to help me.* With that realization I closed my eyes and slept soundly.

As the first rays of dawn spilled through the blinds, I woke and managed to roll out of bed and walk to the bathroom. I felt drained but also, somehow, energized.

Geoffrey was fixing his tie when he saw me. He pressed his hand against my forehead. "Honey, you're not hot anymore," he said, surprised. "Still, I want you to get back in bed. I'll give you a call later."

He hurried off to work, and I splashed some water on my face. That's when I remembered. *Angels were here last night!* Again, I had the distinct impression that the angels had been with me all my life, that they would always be with me.

A week later I had the surgery. Just as I was waking up in post-op I again saw angels, floating among the curtained cubicles, observing patients. They didn't come to me or even look my way, but I knew intuitively that was because my crisis had passed. Later, the doctor came to give me the good news.

"It looks like we caught the cancer just in time, Robin. I think you'll make a full recovery. You're very lucky."

Three cancer-free years later I know I've been more than lucky. I've been blessed. My recovery from cancer is only part of it, though. I carry with me now the conviction that God's light shines on us always, and never more brightly than in our darkest hours.

A Loving Lullaby

by Delilah LaViano

Another day over, I thought, sighing, as I drove out of the parking lot at work that evening. On the nearby Santa Ana Freeway cars sped by, the drivers all eager to get where they were going. Not me. I was just heading home to an empty apartment. In the three years I'd lived in southern California, I'd found it impossible to make friends—true friends, I mean. I'd met some interesting people, but I couldn't find the real companionship I'd known elsewhere. I missed my family. My husband and I had separated and divorced. Everyone was far away: my friends, my mother in Arkansas, my sister in Georgia and my daughter in Michigan, beginning life on her own. Where did that leave me?

Thinking I wanted some independence and adventure, I'd come out west. My parents had always said we were a can-do family, and I tried to keep up a positive front. Only God knew the loneliness that threatened to overwhelm me. I certainly wasn't looking forward to another night alone in my tiny apartment.

I turned on the car radio, searching for music. I had loved music since I was a young girl, playing piano for the choir in my church. These days it seemed to be the only thing that would bring me some relief.

Some time after I got home, my phone rang. It was Mary, a woman from the Bible class I'd been attending. Mary had no family, and we had once talked about feeling alone. "Sometimes, it's more than I can bear," she'd told me. It helped knowing she understood what I was going through.

"What can I do?" I asked her. "I'm having a bad night. Another one."

"Ask God for comfort," Mary said.

"I've tried."

"Ask Him specifically for comfort," Mary responded. While studying the Scriptures, she said, she had become aware of the many times *comfort* appears in both Testaments. She reminded me that the

Holy Spirit is often called the Comforter. "Now when I pray I concentrate on those passages," she said. Before we hung up Mary said a lovely prayer for me. Feeling a little better, I got ready to turn in.

My bedroom was just large enough to accommodate a record player on a stand wedged between the door and the closet. Every night I put on a favorite long-playing record album to help fill the silence while I drifted off to sleep. I put the needle on the record and climbed under the covers. As the first song began to play, I did what Mary said. *Yes,* I prayed, *bring me comfort.*

The moon spread a blanket of silvery light across me. I fluffed my feather pillow into a welcoming cradle and tried to relax, listening to the music, watching the spinning turntable. Spinning and spinning, just like my life.

My room was filled with music, and I wanted to lose myself in its embrace. Glancing at the record player, I saw what seemed to be black dots rising out of it. After I focused I realized that the dots were music notes floating into the air! I lifted my head to get a better look. The notes rose from the spinning record toward the ceiling. More and more of them filled the room, the very notes from a page of the music being played.

I looked up. The ceiling seemed to open like a window. Two figures descended, each alighting on one side of the record player, facing my bed. They appeared to be men—angels without wings—dressed in soft, white garments. They were taller than the doorways, and their wavy, snow-white hair touched their shoulders. I knew with certainty that I was not dreaming.

Each stretched a muscular arm toward the other, and a large white sheet appeared between them. In one fluid motion the angels grasped the edges of the sheet and stretched it out flat. The music notes immediately spread across it in a pattern. The angels walked slowly alongside my bed, the sheet fluttering weightlessly behind them. They let the sheet drift down and cover me, then they fit the edges under the mattress, gently tucking me in.

Without a sound they strolled out the bedroom door. Somehow the wall became transparent, and I saw that my living room was filled with angels! I heard no words, but I could see their mouths moving in conversation. I felt like a child, lovingly put to bed while the grownups stayed up for a while longer. Feeling protected, I quickly fell into a dreamless sleep while the music continued to play.

I awoke renewed, although my life hadn't changed in those few short hours. It would be four more years, in fact, before I left California for Atlanta, where my sister lives, and where I found fulfilling work. Even now, on occasion, those feelings of loneliness return. But ever since the night I was wrapped in soothing music, I have known God and His angels are my constant companions.

I throw myself down in my chamber, and I call in and invite God and His angels thither.

~ John Donne

ANGELS IN THE CITY

Something about a big city feels threatening. So many strangers carrying so many secrets. So many streets and alleys to get lost in. Does one more person—do I—make any difference in the rush of the crowd? Is anyone watching out for my well-being? Would anyone even notice if I disappeared? Yes—the angels notice.

Subway Sentinel

by Evelyn Fehlberg

New York City can be exciting and scary all at once. I discovered this when I was a freshman at a design school, getting to know the Big Apple. After commuting from my parents' home in Irvington, New Jersey, for a while, I'd found a tiny apartment in Greenwich Village.

One Sunday evening in January I was waiting for the subway at West Forty-Second Street. The station was deserted, and it made me uneasy. I was used to seeing the platform bustling with people. *It's the weather,* I thought, hugging myself against the freezing cold. *Where's that train?*

I glanced at the stairs, hoping another passenger would appear. Most of the time I wasn't afraid in the city. "There's no problem here," I would tell myself if I felt nervous in a crowd or walking alone on a dark street. "God is always with me." It usually worked. But not that night. That night was creepy.

Finally I heard the rumbling and roaring of an arriving train. The loud noise sounded like music to me. The train doors slid open, and

I stepped aboard with a sense of relief. But the subway car was empty too, and I felt anxious all over again. I chose a seat near the door. *Only three stops to Greenwich Village.*

A man entered my car at the next station. He stood looking around for a moment, and then as the doors closed he took the spot right next to me. *God is forever by my side,* I tried to tell myself.

The man sat calmly, staring straight ahead as the train began to move. He wore a knit hat pulled down over long, shaggy hair, and a scarf draped his shoulders. He wasn't a large man, but I was much smaller, and no match for him if he wanted to harm me. "You don't know this," he said quietly, "but I'm your guardian angel."

What should I do? I thought frantically. *I'm trapped on the subway with a crazy man.*

Wham! The door between the cars slammed open. A gang of teenage boys stormed in, maybe nine of them, walking single file, shouting and cursing. They punched each other in some macho display and kicked the seats as they swaggered down the aisle.

Trembling, I stared at my lap, clutching my purse. These guys were looking for trouble. The man sat silently beside me. When the gang passed in front of us, one of them said, "Aw, there's nobody in here!"

They left the train at the next stop, and the man patted my hand. I wasn't sure what to say when we both got off at the station in Greenwich Village. My guardian immediately blended into the crowd on the platform. But the One who sent him would forever be by my side.

Mystery of the
Missing Report Card

by Pamela K. Keyser

*W*ith every nerve in my body tensed, I hurried down the dark streets of San Francisco's Mission District. Frightening even in the daytime, the neighborhood took on a sinister life of its own in the early morning hours. Only an emergency would have gotten me into those filthy alleyways at 2:00 A.M., and that was exactly why I was there that night. Clutched in my hand was my third-grade report card. It had to be signed for school the next day— "No excuses," my teacher had warned. So I *had* to find my mother.

I reached the back door of another loud, smoky bar and pushed it open. Inside I stood for a long moment, giving my eyes a chance to adjust to the dim light before I scanned the bar. *Not here.* I slipped out and continued down the garbage-strewn streets.

Teacher's words ran through my head: "No tricks this time, Pamela Parton. Understand?" Every six weeks we got our report cards, and every six weeks those cards had to be signed and returned the day after. It had taken me a month to return the first one, and each day, in front of the whole class, Teacher made sure to remind me of it. The next time around I had signed the card myself. "Did you think you would get away with this?" she had demanded, brandishing the stiff card with my mother's name childishly printed on it. The class had snickered at my failure at this simple assignment. How hard could it be to get your mother to sign a piece of paper? None of them knew that drugs and alcohol could make it impossible.

Gripping the card in my hand, I considered my options. There was only one bar left, a biker hangout everyone called the Harley-Har-Har Bar. I peered down the alley and hesitated. The passageway was two blocks long and dark; anything could be lurking in it. But the open street would take twice as long. *Better to get it over with.* I took a deep breath and started down the alley.

About a third of the way through, I heard heavy footfalls behind me. I looked over my shoulder. In the murky night I could just make out the gigantic figure of a man standing in a boarded-up doorway. He was as tall as the doorframe, almost as broad and dark as night itself.

I took a few steps forward. The footsteps followed. I walked faster—so did he. I started running, my arms pumping as my feet flew over the debris that littered the alley. Then I heard the thunder of his shoes right behind me! In the next instant I was dangling in midair, held up by the back of my shirt, my feet thrashing uselessly. Slowly I was twisted around, like a spider hanging on a thread, to face the man who had caught me. His blazing brown eyes pierced me like lasers. The veins in his neck twisted into steel cables.

"What're you doin' here?" he snarled.

I opened my mouth, but not a sound came out.

"Come on," he growled, tucking me under his arm like a rolled newspaper and carrying me back the way we had come. I lay limp in his grip, too frightened to move. And then I realized my hands were empty. The report card! Had I dropped it in the alley? *It doesn't matter now,* I thought, wondering what terrible thing was going to befall me. And who would care anyway? No one was looking out for me. I'd heard an old man on the street once talking about God in heaven, who watches over us. *God, are You watching me now?* I asked.

When we reached the sidewalk the man jerked me out from under his arm. "Stand up, girl!"

I locked my wobbly legs and waited. The man bent down toward me. "You listen to me, white girl," he roared. "I'm gonna give you some change, and I'm gonna put you on the bus. And I don't *ever* want to see you in this part of town again! You hear?" I nodded. I didn't care what Teacher did to me. I would never go looking for my mother around here again. Then a city bus materialized behind the man like a moving island of light. It was my bus, the one that would take me home.

The clock read 3:30 A.M. as I crawled to my hidden bed behind the living room couch. I couldn't chance sleeping out in the open at my house. I could never be sure who was going to end up spending the night.

The next morning I was surprised to see my mother at home. I sat beside her on the bed and took one of her trembling hands in mine. I told her all about what had happened the night before. My mother twitched on the bed, but once in a while she focused her green eyes on mine and tried to smile.

"So I'll probably get in trouble again for not having my report card," I finished.

"You're lying," a voice behind me sneered. "That's the dumbest story I ever did hear!" Spice, my mother's boyfriend, stood laughing at me from the bedroom doorway. "I'm from that part of town, and ain't no man there as big as all that!"

I grabbed my satchel and took off for school. What did Spice know?

As the other students chattered around me in the classroom, I sat at my desk, dreading the moment I would have to reveal that I didn't have my signed report card—again. "Okay, students," Teacher said. "Please come up as your name is called." I hugged my book bag to my chest as, one by one, my classmates put a signed report card on top of her desk.

"Parton!" she called.

I squeezed my satchel closer to my chest. Not hearing the expected footsteps, Teacher snapped her head up and looked at me over her half-glasses.

"Parton!" she repeated. "Your report card."

Instinctively, I nodded and opened my book bag, pretending to look for the report card as I tried to come up with an excuse. My hand rummaged over the contents of my bag: schoolbooks, an orange peel, a broken barrette, my Ginny doll and—*what's that?*—a square of thick folded paper.

The class had fallen silent. Teacher stood. My hand closed around the piece of paper. *I'll tell her I grabbed this in the dark this morning instead of my report card!* I thought, pulling it out of my bag.

I swiped my tongue over my dry lips to begin my lie and unfolded . . . *my report card!* "I got it! I think," I stammered, holding the card out in front of me as if I were offering a bone to a snarling dog.

"Well, bring it up here!" Teacher commanded.

I went to her desk, laying the bent manila card on top of the pile.

"It *is* signed, isn't it?" she said, eyeing me over those glasses.

I looked down at the card. There on the signature line was the light cursive writing of my mother's signature. I stared at it in wonder. "Yes," I whispered. "It is."

Behind me, I heard a few giggles from the other kids. "Well?" Teacher asked, frowning. "Anything else?"

"No, ma'am," I said.

"Then take your seat, please."

I smiled to myself as I walked back to my desk. Teacher didn't know a miracle had happened. And the signed report card was only the half of it! God had sent me an angel in that dark alley. Not a beautiful, gossamer-winged creature I might have returned to look for, but an imposing giant sure to shock some sense into me, and make me think twice about coming and going whenever and wherever I pleased. I was only a child, after all, and since there was no adult around to remind me of that, God's angel had stepped in to do it.

Not long after, I was taken away from my mother by the state. Eventually I was given to my father, who sent me to live with relatives and friends. People often wonder how I survived. Simple: I was on my own from a very early age, but I was never, *ever* alone.

EATH'S DOOR

"My times are in your hands," says Psalm 31:15. When the physical body is in such distress that life itself teeters on the brink, only God knows whether "it's time" for the soul to depart or remain. Being deathly sick, Rose Rocque and Bethany Withrow glimpsed and heard music from another world. Their lives have never been the same.

Symphony of the Stars

by Rose M. Rocque

I knew I should be asleep, but I sat up on the operating table completely awake. The doctors and nurses didn't seem to notice. They worked frantically over the body of the seven-year-old girl who lay in an operating room in Elmhurst Memorial Hospital in Villa Park, Illinois. It was my body being operated on, but somehow I was no longer in it.

By that summer, years ago, I'd been in and out of the hospital for a year because of spinal meningitis, and this was my third operation for mastoiditis, an infection of a bone behind the ear that's especially dangerous for children. A doctor had given me ether, but after my mind swirled into oblivion, I suddenly woke up. Or at least I was conscious of what was happening around me. I watched an Asian man sitting next to the operating table squeeze a black bag that made funny gasping sounds. An arrow on a round thing with numbers raced clockwise and back. I was fascinated.

Then I saw someone else: A tall man with a short beard and shoulder-length hair stood beside me. His eyes shone like my mother's sapphire wedding ring. His clothing, a long robe, was lit up, as though by hundreds of flashlights. The doctors and nurses were very busy, and I could tell I was the only one who saw him. I knew he was there to take me to heaven, just as I had asked. But he had no wings!

Every morning for weeks I had cried when I heard the doctor and the nurses coming down the hall toward my hospital room, dreading what would come next: Two nurses would hold me down while a doctor inserted a needle behind my ear. I always screamed until the painful procedure was over. I was so weak I couldn't even sit up or turn my head. I had given up asking to go home to my little brother, given up dreaming of escaping from the hospital. Instead, I prayed to go to heaven.

I had expected God to send someone who looked like the picture I'd seen in a Sunday school booklet: a winged angel with long blond hair and a flowing gown. Why had God sent me this man with a beard and no wings?

The bearded man did not open his mouth to talk, but I knew he understood my question, and I understood his thoughts. "I come from where God is, and I will take you to Him," he told me. "I don't need wings."

He lifted me in his arms as if I were a feather, and we slowly rose toward the ceiling. I could see the operating room below and the doctors and nurses hovering over the skinny child lying on the table. It was I, but I was also with my angel.

The ceiling above us dissolved like fog and we glided through it, past a closet with green operating gowns folded on shelves. We went through a hallway where a nurse sat on duty. "Ha, ha!" I chortled. "She can't see us!"

The angel carried me into an old man's room. Three women and two men stood at the foot of his bed, looking sad. One of the women was drying her tears with a tissue. Somehow standing in the wall behind the old man's bed was another angel, with shining eyes and clothes that also glowed like hundreds of flashlights. His hair was long and gray. He just stood there, waiting patiently, waiting for something. I didn't know quite what.

Where are Mommy and Daddy? I wondered. My angel carried me down through several floors into another hallway. There on a wooden bench sat my parents. Daddy was leaning over, elbows on his knees, face in his hands. Mommy wiped her tears with a white handkerchief trimmed in lavender. I reached out and touched her cheek. *They should be clapping their hands with joy,* I thought. I was finally going to God's heaven!

"Good-bye," I shouted. "I'm going up!"

Swiftly then, the angel carried me past many floors and out through the roof of the hospital. The farther we went, the darker it became. We flew through the stars and I heard wonderful music that sounded like "sympathies" (which was the way I pronounced the word *symphonies* as a child). I had often listened to Mommy and Auntie playing classical duets on the piano, and I listened to "sympathies" on the radio. But this music was even more beautiful. There were chimes and choirs, and notes that were higher and lower than any on a piano. The music surrounded me like the stars, and it seemed so textured I thought I could touch it. I was embraced by its beauty, and I felt comforted.

We went past the Milky Way with swirls of clouds moving slowly in different directions. Daddy had shown me this galaxy many times, and I recognized it in the night sky. When we sped through a black place where there were no stars, I was not afraid. I was safe with my angel. Soon I would be in heaven, just as I had asked.

Then I saw a world that looked like my globe bank at home. Without sun or moon, the world was lit up like a lamp. As we came closer the brown areas changed to green. The bearded man set me down in a garden and stood behind me.

I looked around with delight at birds and rabbits, trees and flowers such as I had never seen, with colors that weren't in my watercolor paint box. I was happy, I felt no pain and I could still hear the music of the stars.

Where is Jesus? I wondered. I heard footsteps and felt great love around me. I turned my head and was blinded by a huge, white light. I couldn't see anyone. Then I heard a voice: "My child, you must go back."

Go back? No! Not to pain and operations, not to the hospital. I didn't want to go back to earth. I closed my eyes, silently pleading, *I want to stay in heaven forever.*

When I opened my eyes, I was lying in my hospital bed. My parents were standing around me. Two doctors and a nurse looked on.

"May I have some pancakes?" I asked. Everyone looked startled. "May I *please* have some pancakes?" I said louder, sitting up.

The adults suddenly moved in different directions. Mommy took me in her arms, and Daddy knelt by the bed and cried. Before long a nurse handed me a tray with a plate of steaming pancakes, and I wolfed them down. I was kind of mad at God for sending me back to this awful hospital, but seeing my parents so happy made me happy too. I knew I could stop praying for my life to be over. I was finally going to get well and go home.

Years later I learned that my heart had stopped on the operating table, and the doctors had to massage it externally for forty-five minutes before it began to beat on its own. I was left with some handicaps from my illness, but my childhood was filled with my family's love, and my memory of God's "sympathies" has always sustained me. I heard the music, and I know heaven is real. Someday my angel will take me there again.

On the Brink of Heaven

by Bethany Withrow

All night the pounding of my heart kept me drifting in and out of sleep. Now, on a frosty December morning, I pulled myself from underneath the warm blankets with great difficulty. Every day, it seemed, I awakened more exhausted than the day before.

Eight years earlier, at seventeen, I had been diagnosed with lupus erythematosus, a degenerative systemic condition that produces a range of debilitating, sometimes mysterious, symptoms, including arthritis. For months I had been battling a severe flare-up that kept me prisoner in my house—except for stays in the hospital when I had fever as high as 106 degrees. As a result of steroid drugs, I developed diabetes. Today I felt worse than I had in months.

Even breathing was painful. But something stranger was happening. When I touched my face, it felt unusual. I hobbled to the bathroom mirror. Staring back at me was a face I hardly recognized. It was horribly swollen, and my left eye drooped.

"Butch!" I called to my husband. He took one look at me and ran for the phone. "I'm calling the doctor."

Dr. Alexander told him to bring me right over. My husband had been by my side through many lupus crises, so to see him this unnerved scared me. *Maybe I've suffered a stroke.*

In the living room, as I struggled with my coat, a flash of brown through the window caught my eye. There in our wooded yard stood a baby white-tailed deer all alone. *How strange he came this close,* I thought. Our gazes met and lingered. I love animals. Suddenly, with a graceful little jump, he was gone. But the sight of him had calmed my spirit.

We were almost out the door when my mom called from Wichita, Kansas, to check on me. I could tell how worried she was. Mom used to say she asked God for a "hedge of angels" to protect her children. I reminded her to ask God to keep His angels close to me this day.

Lupus is a disease of many guises, and Dr. Alexander couldn't determine what was wrong with me or how to treat it. He took X rays and drew blood, then sent me home to rest. "Keep still and call me immediately if you get worse, Beth," he said. I knew he was trying to spare me another traumatic hospital stay. Unless my condition was life-threatening, I wanted to be at home.

In the car I studied Butch. I knew he hated leaving me to go in to work. He walked me inside the house and made sure I was comfortable on the couch. Then, as he leaned over to kiss me, I felt a tear fall on my brow. "Don't worry," I whispered. "I'm going to be all right."

But the symptoms worsened. I tossed and turned on the couch, my heart thundering. Late in the day I finally tried calling Dr. Alexander but couldn't reach him. I was getting weaker. I talked to Mom again, and she said she and her friends at church were praying for me for all they were worth. After we hung up, Mom was so worried she called my father, who lives near me in Virginia. He came over to check on me and wasted no time getting me to the hospital.

By midnight I was once again in intensive care, hooked up to oxygen and a slew of beeping, blinking monitors. Butch had taken up his familiar position in a recliner by my bed, while doctors and nurses paraded in and out of my room. Eventually, around 3:30 in the morning, the traffic slowed. Butch nodded off while holding my hand, and I thought I was falling asleep too. Then I realized something altogether different was happening to me, something both wondrous and fantastic.

I drifted in a smoky grayness, not quite floating and not quite walking. I was free of all the medical equipment I had been tethered to moments before. I traveled down an extended passageway. It felt like being inside a telescope; in the dim distance I discerned a glow. With amazement I realized I was no longer in pain. I moved effortlessly toward a radiant, golden light. As I drew closer, I noticed a beautiful figure within the light, standing with outstretched arms. Indescribable peace flooded my senses; the feeling expanded the closer I came to the figure emanating from the light.

All at once I knew I was in the presence of the Son of God. Angels were everywhere, flying to and fro as they hastened to do the Lord's work, each encircled in its own golden bubble of light. Their flowing gowns were translucent, and their features were serene, noble and wise.

I was aware of Jesus communicating directly with me, though no words were uttered. His language flowed through me. He told me not to be afraid, that He wasn't ready for me yet, that I would be going back: *There are still things for you to do and songs for you to sing.* An overpowering sensation of being loved seized me. I felt a joy I had never felt before—the full experience of Christ's love for me.

Suddenly, as if a curtain had been drawn back, I found myself amidst breathtaking surroundings: magnificent mountains, rolling pastures, singing brooks. I saw a distant red barn and I was happy; this meant there were animals in heaven. I thought of the baby deer I had seen that morning and all the animals I loved.

I noticed a man and woman standing behind Jesus and angels hovering and singing above them. I recognized the woman as my grandmother, who, before she died the previous year, had been doubled over with osteoporosis. Now she stood straight and tall, holding the hand of my granddaddy. He died long before I was born, but I had seen many pictures of him. In his free hand he held a bowl.

I knew what it contained. Mama loved to tell about her daddy's prowess in the kitchen. On Saturdays Granddaddy reveled in making his special chili, full of secret, savory ingredients. That bowl contained Granddaddy's Saturday-night chili, and far from seeming irrelevant or bizarre, this fantastic detail reassured me that my grandparents were happy, together again in their love. It told me that heaven was a place God has made for each of us.

Then Jesus was communicating with me again. "I have given you a special husband, and I have given him strength so he can care for you." I was always aware that Butch was unique; now the words of Jesus filled me with pride and gratitude.

He reminded me once more that there was much left for me to do; then I was zooming backward through the telescopic passageway as if time had been reversed. Almost instantly I was in my hospital bed again, reattached to the monitors and oxygen. But I was not disappointed. I was thankful and brimming with joy.

Immediately I wanted to tell Butch all about my amazing experience, but he was sleeping so peacefully, I did not have the heart to disturb him. I wondered why the monitors hadn't sounded an alarm while I was gone. My journey had seemed to last a long while. God's time, though, is different; what feels to us like hours may be only a blink of the eye in heaven.

For the first time since returning, I looked around the room, and there they were: angels, angels everywhere, flickering like candlelight, hovering protectively around us like a hedge—a hedge of angels.

No one sleeps late in the hospital. Soon the nurses and doctors were busy, and Butch woke up. I told him my experience, and he listened intently, stroking my hand, never doubting for a moment that what had happened to me was real.

All that day things looked markedly different, as if a bit of the light I had seen now touched and infused everyone and everything I encountered. I continued to sense the presence of heavenly beings in my room. Even Butch seemed to have an angelic glow about him.

The doctors were amazed to see that the swelling in my face had gone down and the position of my eye was back to normal. They continued running tests for the next few days, including an MRI. When they slipped me into the cylinder for that test, it was like being back in the heavenly passageway, and again I saw the angels. In the waiting room before the test, a frightened little boy was waiting his turn. I saw an angel hovering over him. I told him what I saw, and he became calm.

At last Dr. Alexander said I could go home. "All we know, Beth," he reported, "is that you suffered a major lupus flare-up and now you're getting better. But you were very, very sick." Then, smiling, he said, "Don't scare me like that again!"

I don't want to scare anybody, because I know from my journey that there is nothing to fear when we are with God. He protects us and loves us at all times. Full awareness of that love is the greatest healer of all.

Nothing about life has been the same for me since I saw the angels.

I no longer have to take insulin, my fever is gone, my heart beats normally. I still have lupus and I get sick, but it is not as bad or as terrifying as before. Now I have a continual sense of life's secret beauty.

I finally sat down and told Mom the whole story, and she cried tears of elation that her parents were happy with God, and that a hedge of angels protected her daughter.

Yet angel-echoes reach us,
Borne on from star to star,
And glimpses of our purchased home,
Not always faint and far.

~ Frances Ridley Havergal

ANGELS IN THE

EVENING

In the evening it's so easy to lose hope. The transition between day and night mirrors the link between the past and the future. We let our painful "yesterdays" color our unknown "tomorrows" and the fear can paralyze us. Remember, you are not alone; your angels are watching throughout the evening, into the night.

Which Way Now?

by Fred A. Aiken

When I was in school, I loved to hike, especially with my friends from the Grove City College Outing Club. We had a cabin on state game lands near Kennerdell, Pennsylvania, and I'd explored a lot of the area. But that December day thirty-five years ago I decided to go on a late-afternoon trek into unfamiliar territory. My plan was simple: Head north till I got to the stream, follow it to the Allegheny River, then go south till I came to the bluff with the well-marked trail back to the club atop it. *I'll make it in time for supper,* I told myself.

But the going was slow. My boots sank nearly ankle-deep in the muck on the bank of the stream. I had to go through dense brush; at times it was so thick that I had no choice but to ford the stream and continue along the other side. I pressed on, knowing once I reached the river it would be an easy hike to the bluff. When I heard the rumble of the Allegheny in the distance, I gave myself a pat on the back, proud of my skill as a woodsman.

As I got closer to the river I saw a man sitting cross-legged on a boulder. He wore a red-and-black plaid hunting jacket with matching hat, and he had a rifle in his lap. When he heard me approaching, his head jerked up. "Thank God," he said. "I'm so glad to finally see someone! I'm lost. I've spent most of the day trying to find a familiar marker. Can you help me?"

"Sure," I told him. He looked exhausted, and I could tell by the way he wolfed down the chocolate bar I gave him that he hadn't eaten in quite a while. "Why don't you follow me?" I said. "There's a trail on a bluff not too far from here. I can take you to the cabin where I'm staying."

"Thank you," he said. We headed down the old logging road.

Finally we got to the bluff. "The trail's up there," I said.

"I can't climb that!" the hunter rasped. He sat down and put his head in his hands. I walked over to him and put my hand on his shoulder. He turned to face me, his eyes red-rimmed. "Is there any other way?" he asked desperately.

"But our cabin is only half a mile away once we get to the top of the bluff," I began. Then I took a good look at the hunter. He was an out-of-shape middle-aged man who'd been lost in the woods all day. The climb would've been tough for a young, fit college kid like me; it would be impossible for him. "Well," I reconsidered, "I know an easier trail south of here. It would add hours to our trip, though."

"Please, let's just take it," he said.

I hadn't been on that trail in two years, and with night coming on I was reluctant to try to find it. But this hunter wasn't going to get out of the woods on his own. "Okay," I agreed. He stood, and we headed south.

Clouds gathered in the distance, standing out against the brilliant red of the setting sun. By the time I found the trailhead, it was getting dark and it looked like snow. We passed some familiar landmarks—a rusting Model T Ford and the remnants of a colonial-era furnace. I smiled, pleased that I remembered the trail after so long.

It led us right to a raging stream. The water was deep, but there were stepping stones spaced two to three feet apart. As I climbed onto the first, it teetered under me. I nearly fell into the rushing water. Heart pounding, I jumped back to the safety of the bank. "I don't think we should risk crossing here," I told the hunter. "We're going to have to make our way to where the trail picks up again on this side."

The brush alongside this stream was even thicker than what I'd fought my way through earlier in the day. The bank was steep, and when it started snowing the ground got slippery.

I glanced behind me to see how the hunter was faring. He looked like a child trustingly following a parent.

As I turned my head forward again, I stepped on a large rock. It shot out from under me. I lost my balance and pitched down the bank. I grabbed wildly at the brush, thorns tearing into my bare hands. Somehow I stopped before plunging into the frigid stream. I struggled back to my feet and brushed myself off. The hunter looked worried.

Why did I ever lead us this way? I wondered. I felt as if I were blazing a fool's path. To bolster my spirits, I started humming hymns, especially an old favorite that went, "Open my eyes, that I may see glimpses of truth You have for me."

We pressed on, and finally I could make out an old concrete bridge in the distance. We'd gotten back to the trail, which from a spot near the bridge snaked up a hill into a forest of oaks, maples and evergreens.

The snow was coming down furiously, and I could see only about five feet in front of me. Still, the first few switchbacks were easy to find. But as the blizzard raged, the trail disappeared beneath the drifting snow. I walked on blindly until I came to a steep drop-off. *This isn't the right way,* I thought. *Where are we?*

"What's the matter?" the hunter asked.

"I think we should take a little rest," I said. I didn't want him to know I was lost too. He might panic. Sitting in the shelter of a rocky overhang, I reviewed our limited options. We could go back the way we'd come, but it was too far. Besides, the hunter couldn't climb that bluff. We could stay put, but the temperature was dropping and we had nothing to start a fire with. We could keep moving, but I had no idea where the trail was. There was no getting around it. We were in serious trouble.

Cold fear swept through me. I wrapped my arms around myself.

The wind whipped against my neck. Not knowing what else to do, I closed my eyes and prayed. *Dear God, I thought I could get us out of here, but I've gotten us lost instead. Please help us find our way, or we're both going to die.*

A sense of calm came over me. When I opened my eyes I saw a shadowy figure some hundred yards away, standing next to a white pine. I jumped to my feet and ran toward him but tripped over a snow-covered root and fell. When I looked up, the figure was gone.

"Did you see him?" I asked the hunter excitedly.

"Who?"

"The man! Over there!" I said, pointing to the white pine.

"No, I didn't see anyone."

We walked slowly to the white pine. *I'm sure someone was here,* I thought. But the snow was smooth. There was no sign of footprints. I circled the tree, and on the far side of the trunk I saw a faded trail marker.

We went from switchback to switchback, walking for about ten minutes until we lost the trail again. We found another marker. That one was useless, because the tree it was on had fallen and rolled down the hillside. I searched the slope for any evidence of the trail. Nothing.

Which way now, God? I asked.

Then I saw it again, the figure in the distance. It was the strangest thing. It seemed to be a man, but I couldn't make out what he looked like or what he was wearing. He was surrounded by a narrow band of light but somehow remained covered in shadow. The figure turned and headed into the darkness. I followed, confident he would lead us back to the trail. I didn't say anything to the hunter; I knew he couldn't see him. The figure never went too fast for us, and even waited whenever we took a break.

After half an hour we reached a dirt road at the crest of the hill. The shadowy person walked down the road and suddenly stopped. I was about to call out to him, but he just vanished. Then I looked around and realized where we were—a few hundred yards from the Outing Club's cabin.

As the hunter and I ate and warmed ourselves by a fire, I thought of what had happened. My own abilities hadn't been enough to get us out of the woods. Instead, I had to ask God to help, and He sent me a guide.

To this day, if I'm ever feeling lost, I think of that shadowy figure, and I remember the words to the hymn I hummed that snowy night: "Open my eyes, that I may see glimpses of truth You have for me." Then I ask God for His help, knowing that if I follow His lead, He'll always put me on the right trail.

Shall we listen in the sunset,
Listen, listen long . . .
Singing at the sunset,
Angel voices hear.

~ Frances Ridley Havergal

Figures amid the Flames

by Debra Faust

I was putting the final load of clothes in the dryer at about 10:30 that overcast May night. When you have four kids at home, you do a lot of wash. I was beat, and I figured I'd leave the folding until morning. I flipped the door shut and the dryer started with a determined rumble.

The laundry room was on the first floor of our old house, just off the living room, where my husband, Bob, sat watching television. I gave him a pat on the shoulder as I passed through. "Goin' up," I said as he squeezed my hand.

I made my way up the sturdy old staircase to the master bedroom, recently created by knocking down the wall between two smaller rooms. It was in the middle of a paint job. The mattress lay on the floor and much of the furniture lined the hallway. But that night I didn't mind. I just wanted to crawl into bed, wherever it was.

Alicia, age fourteen, said good night and headed down the hall to the room she shared with her sister, Wendi, twelve. The boys—Sean, four, and Dale, ten—shared the other bedroom. I had every intention of grabbing my Bible from the stack of books beside my bed, but I fell asleep almost instantly to the far-off drone of the TV. I must not have been sleeping long, because Bob's voice still came from downstairs when he woke me with a shock: "Deb, the house is on fire!"

I jumped up, alert but a little disoriented. I stepped into the dark, cluttered hallway where I met the overpowering stench of burning wood and insulation. "I can't use the phone!" Bob shouted up to me, his voice seeming to rise on a cloud of thick, billowing smoke. "I'll run next door!"

"Hurry!" I called back. "I'll get the kids."

I rushed to the boys' room. "Fire!" I shouted. "Get up! Fire!" I grabbed little Sean, but Dale slept soundly on the top bunk. I shook him. "Dale, get up! Fire!"

Then I shouted to the girls. Acrid smoke tumbled up the stairs, filling the hallway. My eyes stung and my chest burned. I stumbled toward my daughters' room. Everything was happening so quickly in a chaos of fear and confusion. I still had Sean in my arms. "Everybody out!" I screamed, but the words seemed to bounce back in my face in the engulfing smoke.

I met Alicia coming out of her room. She was dazed and coughing. I took her by the shoulders. "Get Wendi," I told her.

A horrible panic seized me. Blinded and short-winded, I headed back toward Dale's room. I could barely get enough air to shout. I bumped into Alicia again and asked about Wendi. Alicia couldn't speak; she just gagged. Not hearing or seeing anything of Dale or Wendi, I figured they must have gotten out. So with my oldest and youngest, Alicia and Sean, I felt my way to the bottom of the staircase, cringing from the heat and flames shooting out from the direction of the laundry room. Finally we burst through the smoke and out onto the lawn.

I opened my eyes and gulped the sweet night air, pulling Sean and Alicia close. A sprinkling rain began to fall and it felt good on my skin. Bob ran up to us, eyes wide and searching. "Where's Dale?" he asked. "Where's Wendi?"

I screamed their names and frantically looked all around me. Bob ran toward the house.

They're still inside. My babies are still inside!

"Mom," Alicia said, "I'm going in to find them."

"You can't go back in," I said, catching my breath and handing her a crying Sean. "I'll go."

I dashed up to the front door, where Bob was being driven back by the heat and smoke. He grabbed me. "I couldn't get farther than the landing, even on all fours," he gasped. "It's no use. The fire trucks will be here in a minute." I fell to my knees sobbing, feeling utterly helpless. *Please, God, help them,* I screamed inside my heart. *Help them!* Bob and I began to yell, telling Wendi and Dale to follow our voices. My throat burned from the smoke but I kept yelling, my voice hoarse and cracked.

Flames danced through the living room off to my left. I heard glass shattering and a roar like a giant blowtorch. Directly in front of me I could make out the first few steps of the old stairway before it disappeared into an undulating cloud of smoke, tongues of flames lapping its sides. *My children. My children. Where are they?*

Then, in that thick haze, I saw two formidable figures on the stairs. They seemed unaffected in any way by the raging blaze. Such calmness glowed about them that I stopped crying. *Thank You, Lord,* I prayed, standing up. *Thank You.* Time slowed, stilled. My frantic heart grew calm.

Suddenly the figures disappeared. One small hand pushed through the smoke. Dale! His daddy grabbed him, sweeping him into his arms. *Where is Wendi?* Then her hand emerged. I pulled her out and we fell back to the lawn, crying.

The six of us huddled together as if we would never let go, watching as our house went up in flames. Forty minutes earlier I had fallen fast asleep in my bed. Now my family and I were homeless, standing in the rain in our nightclothes. When the fire trucks pulled up, we retreated to our neighbor's front porch.

The old bricks in our house held in the tremendous heat, almost like a kiln, and the fire grew quickly, consuming almost everything. One fireman tried to get in with a hose but his face shield melted. The firefighters said it was one of the hottest fires they had ever encountered. The investigation pointed to the dryer. Apparently, highly combustible lint had clogged the faulty exhaust hose. There wasn't much the firefighters could do to save our home.

Neighbors came to our rescue with jogging outfits to wear until we could buy clothes. People donated food and kept us in their prayers. We spent that first night with our pastor, then a week with friends. After another week in a motel, with the help of the American Red Cross and our church family, we were able to find an apartment until we could rebuild. Clothing poured in, especially for the little guy, Sean. The school went into high gear to replace Wendi's and Dale's instruments so they could play in a band concert that first week. Mighty God reached out to us through the helping hands of neighbors and friends—angels each and every one.

There are earthly angels and there are heavenly angels. The two

magnificent figures that appeared on the fiery staircase that evening were sent by God to save my children, who miraculously escaped the flames unharmed and safe.

When Wendi told me, "Mom, someone pulled me out," we assumed she meant Dale.

"No, Mom," Dale said, "I didn't even know she was there." We're convinced Wendi felt the hand of an angel!

Though destruction walk around us . . .
Angel guards from God surround us.

~ James Edmeston

ANGELS ON THE

ARM

There's more to farm life than nature's beauty. Alongside bounty there can be blight. The rains can turn to floods, the sunshine to drought. And then there's the steel and wheels; farm vehicles and machines pose dangers that can catch even cautious workers off guard. Byron Miller and Anna Marie Robbins know from experience that God's angels are "ever near" the farmer and his family.

Glorious Harvest

by Byron D. Miller

Threshing season was an exciting time when I was growing up on a farm in eastern Kansas in the 1930s. The whole community helped harvest the wheat, working one farm and then moving to another. For two or three days every summer our place was filled with people. All our neighbors came and extra workers were hired for a dollar a day—a dollar more if they had horses and a wagon. It was as if the circus had come to town, complete with giant machines, teams of horses and a constant parade of rumbling wagons.

I was up extra early on those mornings, doing my chores and running through the barnyard with the chickens squawking out of my way. I had favorite perches from which to watch everything, and I dreamed of being old enough to participate. All the farmers used Elmer's steam-powered threshing machine, and I remember seeing it chug-chug-chug up the road, rattling the planks of the bridge as it crossed the Marais des Cygnes River flowing by our farm. Horses pulled open-sided hayracks, grain wagons that looked like wooden boxes, and the wagon filled with water for Elmer's machine.

I remember one harvest better than all the others, and a July day that changed my life forever.

It was already hot that morning as I stood on our screened porch to get a view of the wagons when they first turned into the lane. Later I sat by the well, listening to the men trade stories while they stopped for a cold drink. They laughed at each other's jokes and wiped sweat from their faces with bright-red bandannas. They talked eagerly of a cool swim in the river and of the delicious smells coming from the house where the womenfolk were preparing a feast.

After the men headed back to the thresher, I stood at the well and watched them at work. Dad came by late in the afternoon. "Day's almost over, Byron," he said. I guess I looked disappointed because Dad put his hand on my shoulder and said, "Your mother and I think you're big enough to help on the grain wagon. What do you say?"

My dream had come true! I ran happily beside my dad toward the thresher. The workers wielded pitchforks from hayracks on both sides, tossing bundles of wheat onto a conveyor leading to the belly of the machine. The thresher devoured the wheat, separating the seed and forcing the straw up a chute where it blew into the air and fell down to form a stack on the ground. Grain poured like sand from another chute into the deep, boxlike wagon.

"Your job is to shovel the grain away from the chute as it comes down," Dad said. "Spread it out so it won't pile up and spill over the sides. Your cousin Dick will be here to help." He boosted me up the tall side of the grain wagon.

I stood in the wagon and watched with fascination and pride. Children were not allowed near the thresher. Up close, the machine was huge, a maze of pulleys and belts with the separator at the end of one long belt and the steam engine at the other. It belched black smoke and breathed fire as the engineer fed it with shovels of coal. Dad hitched horses to a full wagon and drove away toward the granary. A hayrack rumbled and squeaked into unloading position, and men tossed the golden bundles onto the creaking conveyor belt. Clouds of dusty straw blew from the chute. Horses snorted and stomped, afraid of the whirring wheels and belts. The penetrating smells of wet leather, coal smoke, manure and sweat hung heavily in the hot air.

Dick arrived and jumped to the wagon floor. We each grabbed a shovel and leveled out the grain as it poured steadily from the chute. Dick said, "You've got the hang of it, Byron. Keep scooping. I'll be back."

Dick climbed out of the wagon, and I continued to shovel the grain and spread it evenly around. It was hot down there in the wagon, and my shoulders began to ache, but I didn't care. I felt good working by myself. I was helping my dad.

The machine roared as the grain cascaded into the wagon, and the light from the setting sun glared into my eyes. The air was thick with dust; I had to squint to see. Wheat beards scratched my neck and arms, but I couldn't stop shoveling because the grain poured from the chute so fast it began to cover my feet and legs. I worked harder, but it piled up faster than I could scoop.

Sweat ran down my forehead and stung my eyes, and when I took a second to wipe my face on my shoulder, I dropped the shovel. In an instant it sank out of sight in the bed of grain. I groped for it, desperate, but it was lost. I tried to spread the grain with my hands, but it poured out faster and faster.

Where was Dick? Where was Dad? Through the haze I could see some men on the rack on the other side, but they were still tossing bundles, and they weren't looking at me. The machine roared so loud no one would hear if I called for help.

Suddenly a dense cloud of straw blew directly into my face. I was blinded. Grain kept pouring out of the chute, piling up all around me; I couldn't push it away fast enough. I couldn't move my legs. I threw my hands over my face, and something deep inside me cried out as I fell forward into the grain.

I'll never know what happened next or how much time passed. I thought I would sink down into the grain like the shovel and disappear forever, but I landed in someone's arms. I felt myself being lifted up and carried to the back of the wagon, where I would be safe. Three strange men were with me, or at least they were like men. The one who carried me gently picked wheat beards from my face. Then he poured water on a piece of soft linen and wiped the pain from my eyes. The other two leveled out the grain.

I wondered if they were angels, but the light was so bright I couldn't see them clearly. One of the three seemed to be in charge, and he somehow got the attention of the farmers by the thresher. The roar of the machinery stopped as someone shut it down.

Then I saw Dad. He climbed quickly into the wagon and grabbed me, holding me close. He seemed worried. He wiped the grain from my face, but his hands were rough and dirty, and his bandanna wasn't soft like the one the stranger had used. I asked him where they were.

"Who?" he asked.

"The three who were with me."

"There was no one with you, Byron. You were here all alone."

After he could see I was all right, he hitched a team of horses to the wagon. As we headed toward the granary, I saw the three again, and one ran to the back of the wagon where I was riding. "This day is important," he said, "but you won't understand it for a long time."

Before I fell asleep that night, I thought of the thresher and the grain and the three who had helped me. I sensed I was different somehow because of everything that had happened. But the next morning, I woke up and ran through the barnyard with the chickens squawking, and I just went about the business of being a little boy.

Years passed before I thought about my experience again—a long time, just as I had been told. I had children of my own before I appreciated that God had sent His angels just for me.

Farmer's Helper

by Anna Marie Robbins

My husband, Charlie, was getting ready to feed the cows over the hill on our Montana farm. It was a chore we generally did together: I drove our pickup while he threw the hay out to the animals from the back of the truck. But on this cold day, Charlie said, "Oh, hon, you just stay here. I'll take the tractor." He was probably right. My arthritis was acting up, and driving the truck would only aggravate it.

From the barn I could hear the sound of the motor as Charlie drove over the gentle crest of the hill then down the steep incline on the other side. Just by listening I could tell exactly where he was. He had started on his way back when I heard the tractor chains spin and grind horribly. Something was wrong!

Afraid to imagine what awaited me, I walked as fast as my stiff legs could carry me. The steady idle of the machine drowned out my thoughts. When I got to the top of the hill, I saw something terrible on the other side. The tractor had spun out on the ice and overturned, and I could make out Charlie, in his old tan coat, lying atop the big machine. I didn't have to go one step farther. It was clear he was dead.

I needed to call 911 before going down to him. I'd never make it back up the steep side of the hill alone. I'd be stranded, helpless. No one would find us.

"I'll be back, Charlie," I whispered. "I'll be back."

I hurried to the house, all the way repeating, *It'll be okay. God, be with me, and it'll be okay.* I dialed 911, then summoned my strength to walk gingerly down the steep hill. This time, I didn't let myself look at dear, sweet Charlie. *God, why did he have to die all alone?* I looked at my feet, concentrating on each tiny step. Not until I got to the tractor did I look up.

Where was Charlie? He wasn't on the tractor at all! He was on the ground, pinned under the big machine. It would have been impossible for me to have seen him from the top of the hill. But if I hadn't seen Charlie, then who?

I reached under the tractor to switch off the motor. In the stillness that followed, I kept talking to Charlie and rubbing his pinned legs through his dark work pants, even though I knew he couldn't feel or hear me. I realized then that he wasn't wearing his old tan coat.

An EMT arrived, then a neighbor. "He died instantly when the tractor flipped," the EMT assured me. "He didn't feel any pain. I hope that's some consolation."

It was. An angel had been right there with my husband, making sure he didn't suffer. And then, looking out for me, the angel borrowed Charlie's old tan coat and arranged it so I didn't go down alone to investigate. The angel was with Charlie, and with me too. Just as Charlie would have wanted.

Lord . . .
Come, with all Your angels, come,
Raise the glorious harvest-home.

~ Henry Alford

GUARD

The popular phrase guardian angel *is never used in the Bible, though Psalm 91:11 describes the guarding role of God's heavenly messengers. "He will command his angels concerning you to guard you in all your ways." The angel guard is usually unseen, but occasionally it is made visible in dramatic ways—just ask Robert Plummer or William Wilson.*

Angel at the Bottom of the Stairs

by Robert Plummer

Growing up in the 1940s, in Columbus, Ohio, I had a lot in common with other ten-year-old boys. I liked ice cream, *Jack Armstrong* on the radio, Sunday school, cowboys and Indians—especially Indians. But I had a terrible secret. I lived in dread of my father, a dread that made me feel I was never safe.

I tried to love my father because I did not know other boys weren't beaten when they spilled a glass or broke a toy. But mostly I feared him. I feared his very shadow.

He was a stocky, muscular man whose roaring voice gave an extra dimension of profanity to the curses he spewed when he had been drinking, which was often. He liked to use a leather strap, cracking it like a lion tamer. A lion tamer rarely lets his whip touch the animals. On me, Dad's strap always left a reminder of his untamable fury. I wondered why my father was so full of anger, and if it were my fault.

When my mother tried to stop him, she learned soon enough that any intervention on her part only provoked greater punishment for us both. We simply tried not to upset him, especially when he was drunk.

One pleasure my mother and I enjoyed together, though, was church. I especially loved Sunday school, where I discovered a Father Who was not frightening but all-loving and all-forgiving, Who had creatures at His command called angels. We were taught He would send them to us in times of need. I thought a lot about angels and what they looked like, and I prayed I would not be frightened if I ever did see one. I spent so much of my boyhood in fear.

I loved to sing in church. At school I could hardly wait until music period so I could throw myself into "God Bless America" and "Battle Hymn of the Republic." I had a strong voice too. If someone had asked me my greatest ambition, I would have answered without missing a beat, "Traveling the world, singing with an orchestra like Lawrence Welk's!" When I sang, I felt free from fear.

Though my father held a steady job in sales, we were not well-off because of his carousing, and he often used debts and the hard hours at work as excuses for his drinking. One September day it all came together in an explosion of rage.

That morning my father reminded me to do my chores, not that I ever needed reminding, for there was the devil to pay if I forgot. After school I cleaned the house and settled into the den to listen to *The Lone Ranger* on the radio. Transported by the sounds of galloping hooves and ricocheting gunshots, I barely noticed my father had come home until I heard him bellow, "Bob, did you do your work?"

"Yes, Pa," I answered.

I hoped he would go upstairs and sleep, but instead I heard his lurching footsteps heading for the living room, followed by muttered curses and something crashing to the floor. My whole body began to quake.

"Get in here, boy!" he roared.

I snapped off the radio, my mouth as dry as dust, and went to my father. His face was flushed and his eyes smoldered ominously.

"You telling me you cleaned this room?"

"Yes, Pa . . ."

"Liar!" He kicked the scattered pieces of a broken lamp across the floor. "What about that mess?" He began to loosen his necktie, a bad sign.

I knew better than to argue. He grabbed me by the collar and dragged me toward the basement door. In one swift movement he reached behind it, snatched his old, heavy leather belt and pulled me down the stairs. I was so scared I could hardly breathe. He yanked on the light chain. The suspended bulb swung crazily and shadows convulsed on the walls. A small length of clothesline hung from a pipe running along the ceiling; my father used it to tie my hands to the pipe so that my feet dangled above the floor. He jerked the back of my shirt up over my shoulders.

"Now," he snarled, snapping the leather belt, "I'll teach you!"

I closed my eyes and braced myself for three nightmare impressions: the crack of the belt as it struck through the air, its flaming sting on my flesh and the smell of alcohol as my father expelled a grunting breath with each furious effort. *Please, dear God,* I prayed, *please save me.*

It was then he came, appearing silently and fully to me—a tall, broad-shouldered, unmistakable American Indian, hair the color of shiny coal hanging down his back over a blue-beaded vest. Everything about him spoke reassurance and peace. I knew God had sent him, and I wasn't frightened. His deep, scintillating eyes searched mine for an instant, then turned piercingly on my father who was at the point of whipping me. I heard a gasp and the belt fell to the floor, its brass buckle rattling on the cement. I turned to see my father cover his face with trembling hands and then stagger up the stairs.

When I turned back, the Indian was gone. But I knew for certain that in one form or another that noble angel would always be there for me.

I don't know if my father saw the same angel I did, or if he saw anything at all. When he came down a few minutes later to untie my hands, he was silent. He never spoke of the incident. And he never laid a hand on me again.

Something happened that night that seemed to open up my life to all the possibilities of God's world. I felt I had been given a measure of confidence I had always lacked, except when I sang. The next morning at school my teacher surprised me with an announcement. "Bob," she said after homeroom, "we've picked you to audition for the Columbus boys' choir this afternoon. Only a few boys get selected. Do your best."

I drew in my breath. The Columbus boys' choir was a local group that had gained national fame. I never dared dream I was good enough to join.

After lunch I dashed home, put on a tie and hopped a streetcar to the school where auditions were being held. The headmaster, Mr. Hoffman, patted my shoulder and straightened my tie. "Show us what you've got, Bob," he said.

In a bright soprano voice I sang my heart out, a Mexican song about a youth who escapes home through a window to find his lady love. A few days later I got the news: I was chosen. I had never known such happiness. For the next five exhilarating years I lived and traveled the world with the choir. We had our own school and held class on a bus when we were on the road. During those five years I grew into a man, one who would be different from my father.

Dad died four years ago, and I pray that he made his peace with God. I don't know if I could have ever fully loved my father, but I have forgiven him, and sometimes that is the only love we can give. I understand him better now, knowing he himself had been horribly abused as a child. What he did to me was what had been done to him.

But it was not what I would do to my two sons. That terrible cycle of violence was finally broken one night when I was ten years old and one of God's angels stepped between me and a leather strap, banishing my fear, giving me reassurance.

Return to Juárez

by William P. Wilson

The guard slammed the barred door shut in the Mexican jail I was visiting that January day in 1980. He walked off, his footsteps echoing down the concrete corridor.

I was locked inside a huge, reeking room. I looked around. There were about a hundred prisoners in the cell. Some of the men were lying on the bare floor, wrapped in filthy blankets; some leaned against the wall; others wandered about. A cold winter light filtered down from a few tiny, grilled windows high up near the ceiling.

I had come to this jail in Juárez to assist a local lay preacher. The two of us stood just inside that room with its penetrating odor of urine and sweat—me, an American psychiatrist from Duke University, and my companion, a Mexican ex-convict turned evangelist. As the preacher stepped toward the center of the room to address the men, I asked him what he would like me to do. "Pray," he said.

The ex-convict began to preach. I could understand only a few words of his colloquial Spanish, and my mind drifted to the surprising fact that I was there at all.

I had been under a lot of stress back home in North Carolina, carrying two careers at the same time: one as a psychiatrist in private practice, another as a professor of psychiatry at Duke. I had taken time off that winter to stay at a retreat ranch friends had told me about near El Paso, Texas. Visitors were invited to take part in the ranch's many outreach ministries. One was to this jail, where, I was told, many of the prisoners were mentally ill.

Perhaps in choosing to come along I was subconsciously trying to work through unpleasant memories from my days as a young doctor. I had taken a junior staff job at a state hospital in North Carolina where there was a ward for the criminally insane. In that ward there had been the same angry faces I was seeing here in this Mexican jail, the same aimless roaming, even the same pungent smell of disinfectant. Some of the patients in that North Carolina ward had been murderers. One man had killed a fellow inmate with his bare hands

51

and constantly tried to maim anyone he could, lunging out to bite, kick or stomp. We doctors never knew when one of the patients might turn on us, and we were glad there were guards nearby.

But there were no guards nearby now. The mentally disturbed prisoners were easy to spot. Rousing themselves as we entered, they uttered gibberish, railed at the two of us, and made obscene gestures. There was no way of knowing which of these men might suddenly become violent.

Many of the prisoners were moving toward us now, some grouping themselves around the preacher, some around me. I became aware of one man in particular, hovering at my left. I turned. From two feet away the man was glaring at me, his eyes narrowed with rage. The fellow was dressed in a stained, torn shirt; his chin jutted forward. I was used to helping my patients cope with their fears, but now I was the one who was afraid.

The man with the angry eyes thrust his face still closer. I edged along the wall, trying to put some distance between us. He followed. For twenty minutes we moved together in a macabre dance, never more than a foot and a half apart, never closer. At last, quite abruptly—it wasn't until years later that this struck me as odd—the poor creature gave up his pursuit.

With relief, I turned my attention once again to the preacher as he gave his altar call to the now quiet room. Some thirty men responded. Shortly afterward the guard came to let us out. I flew back to North Carolina, assuming the whole experience was behind me.

Fifteen years passed. Then I decided to take another break from daily pressures and fly back down to the retreat ranch in El Paso. Once again, perhaps out of some sense of unfinished business, I chose to take part in the ministry of the ranch by visiting the jail in Juárez. As we crossed the Rio Grande into Mexico, I felt the old misgivings.

Soon we were walking with the guard down the echoing corridor to the mammoth cell. Once again the barred door slammed shut behind us, the guard's footsteps faded away and we were locked inside the stinking, ill-lit room. The man with the rage-inflamed eyes was no longer there, but his place had been taken by a dozen others equally restless and angry.

The lay preacher—a different one—began to speak. I took my

place behind him and closed my eyes in prayer. And it was then I saw them.

Through my closed eyes I saw in front of us six magnificent male figures dressed in dazzling robes, whiter than any white I had ever imagined. Each held a double-edged long sword, pointed down toward his feet. I noticed little details, like the fact that the sword hafts were not engraved. The figures were peaceable, and yet there was an aura of overwhelming power about them. They simply stood there looking at the preacher.

For ten minutes, unwilling to open my eyes and bring the vision to an end, I gazed at the mighty figures. I felt a sense of exultation but not of surprise, as if it were in the natural order of things that they should be there. At last I opened my eyes.

The shining figures were still there.

I could see them as brilliantly with my eyes open as with my eyes closed. I wondered suddenly, had they also been in this cell during my first visit, watching, maintaining a safe space between me and that angry-eyed man as he followed me? Were they protecting both me and him from destructive emotions? Could they have been the reason he abruptly gave up and moved away?

One thing was certain: I felt safe now, fifteen years later, knowing the angels were nearby. Bit by bit, as the preacher reached the end of his sermon, peace settled over the cell. In response to the altar call, a score or more of the prisoners came forward. With the dazzling creatures looking on, the preacher and I prayed with each prisoner and the service ended. A guard arrived and opened the door, and we left that beautiful, holy room.

On the airplane back to North Carolina, I thought about the many professional and personal uncertainties that lie ahead as I grow older. I will face them with a different attitude now, knowing that angels are looking on, robed in white, swords in their hands to protect us against the enemies of doubt and fear. I had seen with my own eyes a heavenly resource I had only *heard* about before that day in a Mexican jail.

OSPITAL

A stay in the hospital. For patients and hopeful well-wishers—for the sick and their waiting families—the days are draining. A question weighs heavily: Will health gain an upper hand or will disease or injury "win"? Facing sickness or even death—our own or a loved one's—we are not alone. God's messengers are nearby, some of them looking like "regular guys," with or without wings.

Preparing a Place

by Kathy Deaton Bohannon

I sat outside the intensive care unit waiting for my father-in-law's nurse to come for me. Jack Bohannon—Daddy Bo we called him—was critically ill with a severe heart condition. We'd been in the hospital round-the-clock all week. Now it was time to say good-bye.

Family members were taking turns this evening, each of us allowed only fifteen minutes with Daddy Bo. My husband, John, and his mother had gone first. The door to the ICU swung open, and they came out. "Okay, Kathy," the nurse said solemnly as she led me into the dimly lit room. She stood by the door. *To keep time,* I guessed. How could I possibly tell Daddy Bo everything in fifteen minutes? I moved to his bedside and took a deep breath. "Daddy Bo, it's Kathy," I said, touching his thick white curls that blended into the pillowcase. His eyes opened then fluttered closed. "I love you," I said, and gently squeezed his hand.

Watching as he drew each labored breath, I remembered the things I loved about Daddy Bo. I owed him so much. He had helped John and me build our first house, a wooden-frame Cape Cod set on land John had inherited from Daddy Bo's parents. Daddy Bo had spent hours down on that den floor playing with our son and daughter. He loved his garden and took joy in supplying us with homegrown peppers and tomatoes.

The nurse motioned to her wristwatch. I kissed Daddy Bo's forehead. "I love you," I whispered, "for reasons too many to count."

Leaving the ICU, I fought back tears. *Don't break down now,* I told myself. I wanted to be strong for my husband, my children and my mother-in-law. I hurried to the nearest elevator, hoping to slip away unnoticed so I could pull myself together. Inside the empty car I pressed a button at random. The number eight was lit when I pulled my finger away from the panel. Then the doors opened to a darkened hallway. *Privacy.* Clearly the employees on this floor had gone home for the day.

In the glow of a lone table lamp, I saw two chairs tucked against a wall. I sat down and buried my head in my hands, letting my tears flow. *Lord, please help me. I want to be able to comfort my family, but in my own grief, I am not strong enough.* If I couldn't accept that Daddy Bo was dying, how could I help my family accept it?

I heard a rustling and lifted my head. A man was sitting beside me, a minister. How long had he been there? The sleeves of his long black robe were wide and flowed onto his lap, where he clasped his dark-skinned hands together. I was mesmerized by his serene gaze.

"I know you are hurting, child," he said with a lilting Jamaican accent. He reached over and tenderly clasped my hands in his. "Do not be afraid. I am here to help you." His words were comforting, the richness of his accent even more so.

"You love this person deeply," the stranger said. I barely got out a whispered *yes.*

"You know God prepares a place for Jack," he went on.

I was relieved that he seemed to have talked to the family already and knew what was going on. I didn't want to have to answer a lot of questions. For that matter, I didn't think I could. I nodded as his eyes fixed on mine.

"God prepares a place for all of us, His children," the minister continued. "He knows Jack means much to you and your family.

God knows Jack is in pain. God knows Jack is a good father and grandfather and husband, and He has a special place for such a good man."

The minister lifted his hands from mine. I felt close to him somehow. I hoped he'd told my family what he'd just told me.

A sense of peace washed over me. Just then I heard the elevator doors open. My husband rushed to my side. "I've been looking all over for you," he said, taking me in his arms. "I'm glad you're all right." I realized that I had stopped crying.

"Only because of this wonderful man," I said, turning toward the chairs.

"Who?" John asked. The seats were empty. So was the hallway. John and I walked a ways down, but the offices were still dark. No one had gotten on the elevator, and there was no stairwell nearby. Where had my minister gone?

On the way back to the waiting room, I told John what the minister had said about Daddy Bo and the place prepared just for him. I would keep focusing on that. A place just for Daddy Bo. "Is that what he told the rest of you?" I asked.

"Kathy, I never met the man you're talking about," John said. And neither, I found out, had anyone else in the family. So how had the minister known Daddy Bo by name?

Soon after, Daddy Bo died. What helped me and my family most through our grief was the image of the wondrous place in heaven set aside especially for him, just as the minister had assured me.

After the funeral I called the hospital, hoping the minister might be a chaplain there. No one knew whom I was talking about. The operator transferred my call to the pastoral-care department, and I reiterated my story to a staff member. "There are no ministers with a Jamaican accent on staff. And what's more," she said, "there aren't any chairs or a lamp along that wall on the eighth floor."

But I know what I saw. There had been chairs, there had been light, and there had been an angel who prepared a place just for me, as a reminder of God's promise to prepare a place for all His children to come home to.

Regular Guys ~ with Wings

by Billy Baxter

"Wait till I stop the truck, Steven," I warned my nine-year-old as we pulled into the parking lot of Stonewall Jackson High one gray October evening. I could see his hand poised to fling open the door.

"I know, Daddy," he said. "I just want to make sure we get good seats."

I smiled. Football is big in Manassas, Virginia, and it's big in our family. I'd coached both our boys in the Pee Wee league, and now that my oldest, Shane, fifteen, played left guard for Stonewall Jackson's junior varsity, going to the games was particularly exciting.

I parked, and we headed for the stands, a three-story-high metal edifice in the mist. Steven raced down the concrete walkway and darted up the bleachers ahead of me. "Hey, how about right here?" he called, stopping at a row halfway up.

We wiped off a couple spots on the cold bench, saving a seat for my wife, Connie, who'd join us after work. *I love game day,* I thought. The crowd roared as the Raiders ran onto the field. Spotting my older son's white-and-maroon jersey, I yelled, "C'mon, Shane, go get 'em!"

Just after kickoff two of Steven's friends came by. He jumped to his feet. "Hold on," I said. My youngest is a daredevil, ready to leap headlong into adventure from the word go. I have to keep an eye on him. Today I wanted to concentrate on the game. "You guys stay here. I don't want you running around."

A few plays in, things heated up. Our team was on the opponent's fifteen-yard line. One screen pass later, and it was first and goal. "Want a close-up of the action?" I asked the boys. We hurried down to the edge of the field to see the Raiders drive for a touchdown.

Right before halftime Steven asked, "Hey, Daddy, can I have some money for a hot dog?"

"Sure," I said. "But come right back." He went off with his friends to the snack bar. The boys returned just as play resumed. "Be careful," I called when I saw him running up the bleachers.

"Okay, Dad," he said.

I got caught up in the action on the field, until all of a sudden the back of my neck prickled. *Turn around.*

I wheeled, not quite sure why. Through the metal slats of the bleachers I saw Steven sprawled on the ground, his friends leaning over him. One of the guys was shaking him. I heard a panicky cry, "Get his dad!"

I ran to Steven, lying on the concrete walkway behind the stands. As soon as I saw his eyes rolled back and his jaw locked, I knew he was in trouble. "Call the paramedics!" I yelled. I dropped to my knees beside my son's body. "Please, God, help us," I cried. "Send Your angels to take charge over my boy." I looked up. "What happened?" I asked Steven's friends.

"He slipped on the bleachers and fell through the gap," one of them said, pointing to the highest bench overhead. That was thirty feet up! For a moment the noise of the crowd faded. *No one could survive a fall like that.*

Soon I heard the terse voices of the EMTs. "Careful, he might have a neck injury." They eased him onto a stretcher. "Blood pressure's dropping—fast."

"There's no room in the ambulance," one of them told me. "Follow us in your car."

Fighting panic, I asked a neighbor to take Shane home after the game. "Can you try to reach Connie at work?" I asked another friend.

I floored my truck and beat the ambulance to the emergency room. I called my parents. "I'm at the hospital . . . No, it's Steven . . . He's hurt bad, Mom." When I saw my son being wheeled through the doors, I rushed to his gurney. A nurse grabbed my arm. "We can't let you go with him," she said. "We'll let you know as soon as we have any news."

The air was charged with urgency. Mom arrived and sat with me.

Dad went to get Connie. Within minutes a doctor announced, "We're sending your son to Fairfax Hospital. They've got a trauma center." He tried to prepare us for what we'd see.

But when I caught a glimpse of Steven before they put him in the helicopter, I sucked in my breath. His face was blue, his eyes glassed over. Mom laid her hands on his forehead and whispered, "Lord, send Your angels to watch over him."

Mom rode with me to Fairfax. In the car, we spoke not to each other but to God. "Help him, Lord," Mom pleaded. "Protect my son," I said. Steven had looked lifeless on that gurney. I was afraid he might already be gone.

Dad and Connie and her parents met us at the pediatric intensive care unit in Fairfax. We prayed together as we waited for some word on Steven's condition. His injuries were grave: head contusions, broken rib and collarbone, punctured lung, ruptured spleen. "Your son's in a coma," the doctor said. "We don't know if he's going to come out of it."

I felt as if I couldn't breathe. I had to get out of that room. I ran outside. "Lord," I cried, "I put Steven in Your hands." As my prayers left my lips, my fears began to leave me too. I took a deep breath and felt peace settle over me. I had to believe God would look after my little boy, no matter what.

The days blended together as we watched for some sign that Steven was coming back to us. His eyelids fluttered. His lips formed words, but we couldn't make out what he was muttering. Connie and I didn't leave the ICU. Finally, on the fifth day, I insisted Connie go home and get some rest. She looked about ready to collapse. Late that night I sat alone next to Steven's bed. He started mumbling again.

"What is it, buddy?" I asked. Leaning closer, I heard his words clearly for the first time: "Bobby, Daddy knows . . . Daddy knows."

Who's Bobby? I wondered. *And what is it that I'm supposed to know?* I was mystified, but I was thankful Steven didn't seem to be afraid. And relieved that wherever he was, he at least seemed to be among friends.

In the morning, when Connie and my mom arrived, I went out to get some fresh air. As I returned to the ICU, I heard Connie exclaim, "He's awake!" I ran to my son's bedside.

"Daddy," he murmured. "Daddy, I died."

The back of my neck prickled just as it had at the game.

"Last night you were talking to someone named Bobby," I said. "Who's that?"

"He's an angel."

Connie and I exchanged glances. "You kept telling him, 'Daddy knows,' " I said. "Do you remember what you were talking about?"

Steven shook his head no.

"I heard you talking to Shane too. Did you see your brother?"

"No. That wasn't *our* Shane, it was another angel."

We listened, stunned. "I remember slipping on the bleachers and falling," Steven said. "The next thing I knew three angels were pulling me up. It was weird. I saw myself lying on the ground, and I saw you running over to me, Daddy. I was scared. I didn't want to go with the angels at first, but they said I'd be okay.

"Bobby had brown hair, Shane was blond and Kevin had black hair. They looked like regular guys, except they had wings."

Connie asked, "Where did the angels take you?"

"Into a tunnel. It was dark, so they stayed close. We were having fun racing toward a shining light at the end. But before we got there a big shadow came up. When Kevin chased it away, he fell into a hole. Bobby and Shane and me—we had to lean down and help him out. We finally got to the end of the tunnel. Then I woke up."

"Sounds like some adventure, buddy," I said, clapping my son gently on the shoulder. I couldn't say anything more. I was too choked up.

From then on, Steven's recovery was remarkable. The next morning he was able to walk down the hall. Two days later we got the good news: We could take our son home. That afternoon Connie and Mom sat with Steven while I went to the house to get some clothes for him. They saw his eyes follow something across the room and stop at the doorway. He grinned and waved.

"Steven, what are you doing?"

"Saying good-bye to my angels, Mom."

"They're here?"

"Sure, they've been here in the hospital with me the whole time." Then he looked at the doorway again. "So long, guys. Thanks."

CE

Has anyone ever described an icy winter better than poet Christina Rossetti? "In the bleak midwinter . . . earth stood hard as iron, water like a stone." That breathtaking wonderland can be as treacherous as it is beautiful, endangering limb and even threatening life. Can the cold freeze out God's presence? Hinder God from sending out messengers of mercy? No way.

Lost on the Ice

by William N. Lindemann

Flat on my face in frozen snow, gasping for breath, I knew if I didn't get back on my feet I would surely die. I struggled to my knees and shakily rose—only to be slammed down again by a blast of icy snow. Was the howling Wisconsin blizzard going to kill me?

Two hours earlier, under an overcast sky on that cold January day, I set out hiking across the twenty-five-mile-diameter Lake Mendota in Madison. The frigid air pinched my nostrils but I loved it.

Growing up in Wisconsin I had always explored the outdoors— paddling, climbing, wandering the woods. I respected nature without fear. In my childhood it was because Mother assured me my guardian angel would watch over me. But by my teen years I no longer believed in such fairy-tale stuff. Rebellious and headstrong, I ran away from home. I had convinced myself that I was a man totally in control.

At age nineteen I moved to Madison and enrolled in the University of Wisconsin. On that particular afternoon I decided to skip class and walk across the frozen lake near my apartment house. For my trek I

bundled up in a hooded down parka, heavy logging boots and insulated leather mittens.

The big lake had been frozen for many weeks, and the ice was quite thick, except around the breakwater. As I stood onshore I could see people ice fishing in the distance. I figured it would take about two hours to reach the lake's center, where I would decide whether to continue on to the other side or return home. I created a line-of-sight target and stomped off into the snow.

It was a tiring walk and, getting thirsty, I started eating snow. When I reached the lake's center, the wind had picked up and the temperature plummeted. Ominous clouds formed overhead. Snowflakes whirled around me until I could no longer see anyone on the ice. Soon I was swallowed in a blizzard and had to shield my eyes from the stinging crystals. I wanted to turn back toward campus, but I had lost my bearings.

The gale rose in crescendo. I was snow-blind, engulfed by the driving whiteout that took my breath away. Drawing my hood more tightly around my face, I staggered on, looking down, desperately trying to see my boots and to keep walking toward land in a straight line.

Stumbling on a drift, I fell flat on my face. Trying to rise, I was so disoriented that I fell again. There was nothing to do but crawl. Against the ferocious wind, I slowly worked my way across the snow, stretching one hand out as far as possible, digging it in, pulling my knee up to it, and arching my back in inchworm fashion. Every so often thunderous groans rolled up through the slightly shifting ice.

Despair drained any self-confidence I had left and a sense of doom filled me. I did not know in which direction I was going. I sank my forehead against the ice, finally admitting I was totally helpless. At that moment, I knew if I didn't get back on my feet I would die. "God, if You're out there and want me to live," I cried, "You're going to have to do something!"

Above the howling wind I heard it: a deep warning sound like a foghorn. I looked around, but I couldn't tell where it was coming from. I called out, "Make it loud and clear."

Ooooooommm. This time I oriented myself to the direction of the sound. I realized it had come from the rescue station, which was only blocks from my apartment. As I crawled toward it I heard a voice: *Be careful. Watch out for the breakwater. The water is open and deep.*

I remembered the breakwater near the rescue station and knew if I fell in I would die in seconds. I felt ahead with my hand, dragging myself across bumpy snow and ice. After a while I heard water lapping. Again the voice guided me: *Stay to the right. Climb the concrete wall when you reach it.*

Soon the waves sounded very close, and finally, when I pulled my gloved hand to my face, it was dripping wet. After sliding on my belly to the right, I caught a faint yellow light from the rescue station, a two-story cement structure. The light gave me renewed strength. I worked my way onto the bank and struggled through deep snow to the station and banged on the door with my frozen glove.

The door was pulled open immediately, and strong arms reached out and half-carried me inside. The room was snug and warm. As I blinked away frozen snow, my eyes made out a tall, dark-haired man looking at me. He asked if I was all right.

He said he had spotted me out on the lake and had set the warning horn off thinking it might guide me. He asked if I wanted some coffee.

I nodded gratefully and took the cup he offered, wrapping my icy hands around it, savoring the warmth. I asked him why he was working there in midwinter. He said he was finishing some research. After drinking the coffee and feeling revived, but still too dazed to ask my rescuer's name, I thanked him profusely, walked out the door and made it home.

At the apartment my roommates were curious. I had been gone over seven hours. When I told them what had happened, one wrinkled his brow. "There's no way that rescue station would be open this time of year," he said.

With the taste of the coffee still in my mouth, I replied groggily, "Just a coincidence, I guess." Then I went to bed for a long, deep sleep.

The next morning the storm had passed, and I walked back to the rescue station to find out more about my mysterious benefactor and to thank him properly. The entrance was nearly buried in snow. After

working my way to the door I found a sign affixed to it: CLOSED FOR WINTER. I peered inside through a window and could see that the place was empty.

I couldn't believe it. Someone had been there the previous night! A man had talked to me and served me coffee.

I called the university and was told that the Safety Department ran the rescue station. The Safety Department said the station was closed for the season. Then I decided to telephone the university's Limnology Department, which sometimes does research on the lake water, but they said no one could possibly have been there. As a last resort, I called the Dane County Sheriff's office; they couldn't help me either.

But all the while, growing suspicion told me my search would prove fruitless. For I soon understood who that man in the rescue station was. My mother had told me about him long ago.

Lord, make us aware of the realities we cannot see. Send Your messengers to us today, to help us, to protect us and give us courage, to remind us of Your love.

~ Luci Shaw, from Winter Song

Sudden Impasse

by Charles Ellsworth Smith

My wife, Mary, and I weren't planning the usual turkey dinner with all the trimmings at home that Thanksgiving. Instead, we'd packed our belongings on top of our friends' Econoline van and were heading from Oregon into Washington State. I shared the driving with Buck, while his wife, Jeannie, and Mary rode in back to look after our three young ones. "You drive and leave entertaining the kids to me," Mary said as we headed out.

Although our life together was good, I felt unsettled. It was 1975, and I'd tried my hand at songwriting, run a house-painting business with Buck and had been copastoring a church for a couple of years. Each pursuit had its rewards, but I longed for a clear sense of direction. "What do you want me to do?" I kept asking God. I wasn't sure what was next. So I'd decided to leave everything behind for a while and join our friends on a retreat in the mountains, where we would fast and pray, and live in workers' barracks, pruning pear trees to earn our keep. Maybe while I was away from my daily distractions God would give me an answer.

We drove along the Columbia River and then turned north on Highway 97 into Washington State. Rain started to fall as we crossed the Bridge of the Gods. Buck was at the wheel when we began climbing the narrow, two-lane road through the Simcoe Mountains, heading for Satus Pass, which was more than three thousand feet high. I could hear Mary, Jeannie and the kids singing.

"Hey, will you look at that?" Buck said. "Snow!" The rain had become falling flakes, and as we climbed higher we were soon hemmed in.

"Should we put the chains on?" I asked.

"Not now," Buck said. "Let's get to the top." We had packed the chains, but we'd never expected heavy snow this time of year.

What have I done? I wondered as I stared into the thickening snowfall. I'd taken my family far from home, all because I was searching for direction. Now we were driving in a blizzard on a narrow mountain road.

The snow was a good three inches deep when we reached the top of the hill. Satus Pass has a notoriously steep downgrade, and Buck gently pressed the brake pedal.

"Whoa!" I yelled as the van skidded. There was ice under the snow! Buck tapped the brakes, holding the wheel steady lest he lose control of the van and careen into the mountainside on our right, or over the cliff to our left. We kept sliding, the momentum carrying us over the hill.

"I'll stop as soon as I can," Buck said, working the brakes carefully. We inched our way down the steep incline, still in danger of sliding out of control and over the cliff.

Finally, a hundred yards or so down the mountain, Buck was able to bring the van to a halt. Problem was, we were parked precariously near the middle of the road.

"I'll get help," Buck said, jumping out. He started climbing back up the hill where some cars had pulled over.

"Everything's okay," I said to the women in back of the van, but they heard the worry in my voice. "You all sit tight," I said. "Stay where it's warm for now."

I got out and hurried around to the back, hoping to direct cars around us. As I watched Buck's form blur in the blowing snow, a huge trailer truck crested the hill. It started to descend, looming ever larger as it approached. Almost immediately the truck began to turn sideways. Its trailer was ten times bigger than the van, with wooden-slatted sides, and filled to overflowing with pears from the harvest. The jackknifing truck slid across the icy road, straddling both lanes as it continued relentlessly toward our van.

I ran to the passenger door. I had to get Mary and Jeannie and the children out. I pulled at the door handle. Locked? I could see everyone inside and hear them singing.

I banged on the door. "Get out!" I screamed. I banged on the window. "Hurry!" But it was too late. The truck was barreling broadside down the hill, straight toward us. There was no escape on this narrow road. I knew the decision the driver was trying to make: take his truck over the cliff or crash into the van. I watched him, and

all those pears like a monstrous green mountain, about to crash into us.

I couldn't move. I couldn't save my friends and family. All I could do was pray. Then the driver twisted the wheel to the left, and I saw his face clearly. He had chosen to take his truck over the side. "Lord," I cried, "please protect him—and us."

Time seemed to stop. The face of the driver, the pears loaded on the truck, the snow, the children's singing, all blended into one miraculous moment as an angel of the Lord came between our van and the truck—and in a blinding whirl of white straightened out the truck, guiding it by us with mere inches to spare. I watched with wonder as it safely disappeared through the snow. Then we were helped down the mountain by passing motorists.

I'd thought there were only two ways out of our terrible predicament. From the look on his face, the driver had thought so too. But God had intervened, and I was reminded that His way is filled with possibilities we can't necessarily see or comprehend. I had all the direction I needed: God was in control of every circumstance. I would greet our Thanksgiving in the mountains grateful beyond all my expectations.

ANGELS ON THE

O B

Self-employed or state-employed? Accountant or line-worker? Nurse or nanny? Most of us spend a good part of our days on the job—creating, tending, repairing, sorting, serving, managing . . . the list of possible duties is long. As we carry out the particular responsibility entrusted to our care, we can know that heavenly messengers are also at work, carrying out individual assignments at the behest of their Chief Officer, the almighty God.

Accidental Angels

by Pierre L. Roque

The sun blazed as I roared east on my motorcycle. Sweat stung my eyes and dripped down my neck in spite of the breeze in my face. I felt my energy draining away. As hot as it was on the freeway from Los Angeles, I knew it would be even hotter out near Rainbow Valley. We'd had nothing but sunshine for a long while, and the trees and brush were tinder dry. *Just waiting to burst into flame,* I thought. Fire was on my mind that summer afternoon twenty years ago. I was headed for my job as a correctional officer at a forestry camp run by the California Department of Corrections.

Camp Rainbow housed 105 inmates who had received special training in conservation and fire fighting. The men put in eight-hour days, maintaining wooded areas by cutting firebreaks, removing dead trees and spraying pesticides. But their major job was battling fires, any kind and anywhere from up near Oregon to the Mexican border. My job was keeping the prisoners in line.

After nearly twenty years as a correctional officer, Rainbow was a new assignment. I'd memorized each inmate's name and face immediately. I had to be sure they were accounted for at all times. The other officers and I had an arrangement of three and a half days on, three and a half days off. My job was okay, but staying at the camp was hard, with my wife and children a hundred miles away. "Hey," an inmate said, "you're in prison just like us."

In a way, he was right. I'd known that lonely feeling before. For ten years I'd commuted from the city to another conservation camp. It wore me out, and I asked for a transfer. Then I was assigned to a state methadone clinic in L.A., but when funding was cut back, the clinic closed. I had to earn a living, so there I was at Rainbow. Sometimes it did feel as isolated as prison. While I was in charge of the inmates, who was watching out for my family? Wasn't that my job too? What good was I to them, so many miles away? On those long days and nights far from home, even God seemed distant.

As I pulled into camp on my Honda CX 500 for my first four-to-midnight shift of the week, the commander waved me down. "Brush fire!" he shouted. "A canyon east of Escondido." He'd sent a crew out with only the forestry foreman in charge. All the other men were fighting blazes in other locations, and there were no trucks or buses left in camp. "You'll see the smoke from the fire," the commander said. "Stay on that bike and go!"

I turned my motorcycle around, heading for Highway 15 South out of nearby Temecula. I was already tired from my two-hour ride from L.A., and now I had to climb a mountain. Not easy on a motorcycle, but I had a job to do.

The highway wound south through the towering trees of the Cleveland National Forest area. Beautiful, but fragile. *That's why this work is important,* I told myself. *Keep going.* I could see smoke rising into the sky. I stepped on the gas, urging my bike toward the fire. The smoke was thick ahead of me now. Finally I located a little road leading into the mountains. The men were up there somewhere in a canyon.

I sat for a few seconds to rest, and then I began to climb. My sweat-soaked clothes stuck to my body. The shade from the trees gave me some relief from the sun, but the air was heavy and hot. I could hardly breathe.

Rocks bumped under my front wheel, and the bike swerved.

"Whoa!" I grabbed the handlebars tighter. There was no one on the narrow, winding road but me and my bike. It seemed like the loneliest place in the world. The smoke in the sky above led me like a beacon until I reached the top of the peak. I pulled over to the side of the road.

I squinted, staring into the canyon through the smoke. Success! I'd found them! I spotted the crew working directly below me. There were no flames on the hillside. It looked like they had the fire under control. *Now all I have to do is get down there.*

I twisted the front wheel. That bike didn't want to budge. Suddenly the motorcycle slipped on the rocky road. *Bam!* I was on the ground. In a second, before I could get out of the way, the bike crashed down on top of me. I was just able to reach the kill switch and turn off the engine.

The bike's five-hundred-pound weight was crushing me. I couldn't move! The hot engine pressed into my leg, burning through my pants. If gasoline leaked onto the engine, I'd go up in smoke for sure.

I had to get out! But how? The men were too far below to hear me call. I hadn't seen anyone else on the road. I'd never felt so alone in my life. "Help, Jesus!" I cried. "Please!"

A moment later, around the faraway bend in the road, came an open-top Jeep. The vehicle approached slowly, and stopped within thirty feet of me. A woman in a sleeveless dress stood up on the driver's side. With a winning smile, she said, "Looks like you could use some assistance, sir."

"I sure could."

Then she sat down! *She's going to drive away!* But the passenger door opened, and out stepped the young boy who'd been sitting beside her. He was maybe eight years old, wearing jeans and a T-shirt. He strode over to my side.

The boy reached down toward my motorcycle. What did he think he was going to do? Pull it off me by himself?

But as soon as the boy grabbed the handlebars, I felt the power of his grip. It was as if electricity ran through the frame of the bike! Without a sound, without any effort whatsoever, he lifted the motorcycle. I was free. I crawled out of the way and got to my feet. Reaching for the bike, I set it up on the kickstand. Then I turned to express my gratitude to the woman and the boy.

They were gone, Jeep and all. But where? There hadn't been time for them to disappear around that faraway bend, and the open road was empty in the other direction. Looking down into the canyon, I saw the smoke had cleared. The fire was out, and the men had departed. I climbed on my motorcycle, feeling strong enough to make it back to Rainbow and tend to my injured leg. But I sat for a moment before switching on the engine. A man has to go where the work is, and I realized I'd been doing my job, watching out for my family the best I could. All the while someone was watching out for me too. Even in that lonely place, I hadn't been alone.

Praise to the Lord, Who prospers my work and defends me; Surely His goodness and mercy here daily attend me.

~ Joachim Neander, translation by Catherine Winkworth

Painter's Helper

by Lloyd C. Tohill

My wife, Donna, and I met in the Tidewater area of Virginia when she answered my ad for a painter's assistant. Now, years later, we were living there again. We'd moved back from Oregon, where we'd raised our family on a beautiful ten-acre spread by the Illinois River. I'd owned a cabinet shop, work I really loved, and I'd been studying to become a pastor. A good life, and a dream come true.

But now the dream was shattered. We returned to Virginia so Donna could be near her family. My wife was dying of cancer. I was painting houses again, because it was the only way I could block out my loneliness and despair. Besides, we needed the money.

"God, what good does it do to love You?" I asked, kneeling on the floor to pry open paint buckets in the Norfolk townhouse where I was working that day. I stirred the paint, preparing to touch up any places I had missed the day before. I'd loved God all my life, and I'd done everything I knew to please Him. Now Donna was dying. How could I be a minister? How could I tell anyone of God's love when I could no longer feel it myself?

I stood up and looked around, evaluating the job. I mentally checked off the rooms I'd finished: kitchen, two baths, and all three bedrooms upstairs. I had put semigloss enamel on the kitchen and baths, and flat latex on the bedroom walls, which still had to be trimmed in semigloss.

First I needed to touch up the bedroom walls. I eyed the five-gallon bucket of flat latex paint. Weighing nearly eighty pounds, it was much too heavy to lug around. So I took an empty one-gallon semi-gloss enamel bucket, carefully poured in some of the flat latex and took it upstairs.

A while later I heard a familiar voice call to me from downstairs: "Dad?" It was my oldest son, Lloyd, Jr. I'd asked him to come over from another of our jobs to help me finish here. Things weren't progressing as fast as I'd wanted. I set my bucket of flat latex on the floor and hurried down to meet him. I wanted him to enamel the upstairs trim on the bedroom windows, doors and baseboards with semigloss.

The morning went very well. I enjoyed being with my son, and I liked the thought of him upstairs painting the trim while I was back downstairs working on the walls. At one point, I was busy at the foot of the stairway, listening to Lloyd walking around, opening and closing doors while he worked. When I glanced up, I saw a small man standing at the top of the stairs, though it was more like seeing an outline of a man. He was in profile, facing the bedroom where Lloyd was. The man was translucent, with a vivid, bright gold permeating the upper part of his body.

Oddly, my first impulse was to say "Welcome." But I simply stared for a couple of minutes then looked away. When I looked back, the man was gone.

I completed my work in the living room, but I thought of little besides that translucent man. It had been a startling experience. I wanted to call to Lloyd and tell him what had happened, but I didn't. He just would have laughed.

Lloyd had finished enameling the bedroom trim and stair risers and was now painting two side-by-side doors in the downstairs hall. "Boy, this paint sure dries fast," he said.

The minute the words were out of my son's mouth, I knew something was wrong.

"Lloyd," I said, "you're using a new bucket of paint, right?"

"New bucket? I don't think so," he replied.

I hurried to the hallway and touched the doors Lloyd was painting. Sure enough, they were drying fast. And they were drying as flat and dull as could be.

Flat latex wall paint! He was using the semigloss enamel bucket that was mismarked because I had filled it with flat latex! The whole morning had been wasted! I wanted to yell at him, but I bit my tongue. I should have told him which can to use.

"Well, we'll just have to start over," I said. He put his brush down and went off to clean up for lunch. I'm sure he was upset. "Just a mistake," I called to him as he walked away.

Lloyd didn't answer. "You don't think I have enough troubles, right, God?" I muttered as I headed upstairs to gauge how much re-painting we'd have to do.

Halfway up I could already see the shine on the door at the top of the stairs. *Well, that's okay,* I thought. *We won't have to redo that one.* But then I realized this was the room where my son had been working when I saw the translucent man. I examined the door more closely. It was not only okay, it looked beautiful and freshly painted in semigloss. I walked in and checked the bathroom door. It too was painted in semigloss. The same was true of the windows, baseboards and closet doors. All were done in shiny, fresh-looking semigloss, just as I'd planned.

"Lloyd," I yelled. "Did you paint everything up here?"

"Yes, Dad," he said from the bottom of the stairs. "Everything."

"Did you use the same bucket of paint you were using down there?"

"Yes!"

I walked down slowly and stood close to my son. "Everything up there's been done in semigloss," just as it was supposed to be.

Lloyd looked at me in disbelief. One can of paint. Two different finishes? We hurried over to the two doors he'd been working on when I'd discovered the mix-up. Each of us touched a finger to the surface.

Yup, flat. They were painted with flat latex.

Looking around at the painted rooms, it was obvious my son and I would finish the job on time; very little work had to be redone. But that's because we'd had help—help I knew would be there for us in the difficult days ahead.

ITCHEN

Eating and drinking. These basic elements of life are celebrated from the first to the last pages of the ancient Scriptures. Three angels ate with Abraham. Jesus cooked fish for His disciples. A heavenly table will be set as for a wedding banquet.

Even today messengers of God are present with His people in the daily kitchen tasks and also at memorable sit-down feasts. Just ask Marybeth Weinstock and Thelma Rodriguez, who remember their special visitors.

Elijah's Light

by Marybeth Weinstock

Growing up in suburban Philadelphia in the 1950s, I was lucky to have loving parents who put great value on culture and education. Our home was filled with music and books. It was, however, a more cultural home than a religious one. But when I was eight years old, I was to have an experience that left a lifelong impression on me.

I was a happy-go-lucky kid with an active imagination. Mom and Dad were sensitive to my passion for music and dance, and they enrolled me in an arts camp in the summers. During school months I studied piano and ballet.

My parents prepared me well for the cultural and intellectual side of life, but when it came to questions of the soul, they wanted me to make up my own mind. My mother was an atheist. Her family was not religious and rarely attended synagogue, only on special occasions. My father had rebelled against his strict Orthodox Jewish

upbringing. For many years he had been an agnostic, yet he had great respect, even love, for the cultural aspect of Jewish traditions.

But despite their secular leanings, my parents believed I had a right to my own viewpoint. They decided, therefore, to enroll me in Hebrew school.

We kids all found the Sunday classes at the synagogue tedious, but what appealed to me were the stories of spiritual adventure in the Bible. I loved learning about creation and the great Hebrew leaders, such as Moses and Abraham, and the struggles of the Jewish people. The Bible was my doorway to another world, its tales uplifting and captivating.

"You know what I learned today in class?" I'd ask Mom and Dad excitedly when I got home. "I learned about Moses parting the Red Sea to escape Pharaoh's army!"

"Oh, Marybeth," they'd say, "those are just old stories."

My parents didn't give any more weight to them than they would to a good book. I believed what the Bible said, though I felt uncomfortable talking about it at home, like a child believing in fairy tales. Still, my warm feelings about the Bible and its stories seemed so real.

Then came Passover the spring I was eight years old. I loved the story of Passover, when God led Moses and the Israelites from under the domination of Pharaoh and delivered them from Egypt to the milk and honey of the Promised Land. I had learned in my Hebrew-school classes that for thousands of years the eight days of Passover have been a sacred time of remembrance and faith for the Jewish people.

That year as usual we gathered en masse for the big first-night seder—or ritual meal—at the home of relatives. The second-night seder was a more private affair, just the immediate family in our own home: Dad, Mom, my brother, David, and me.

Leading the ceremony was Dad, who read Hebrew fluently from his boyhood and knew all the proper prayers to be said over the special foods and cups of wine that highlighted the meal. Despite his lack of formal religious commitment, Dad loved the Passover observances. He especially loved its rituals. Mom was drawn in too. The seder always brought us close as a family.

The ceremony touched me deeply. I was elated, especially by the beautiful power of the traditional Passover music we sang.

Then it was time for one more seder ritual: welcoming the angel Elijah into our home as the final cup of wine was poured and blessed. According to the Bible, the mighty prophet Elijah never died but instead ascended in a whirlwind to heaven. Jewish tradition says he became a trusted angelic servant of God. Through the centuries, accounts flourished of how Elijah served in special missions to those on earth in need of comfort, healing or guidance. As the youngest family member, I was thrilled to have the honor of reading the "Four Questions," which help explain the meaning of Passover. And because of my enthusiasm, I was also granted the special privilege of symbolically welcoming Elijah into our home by opening a door for him.

Undertaking my role with solemnity, I rose from my seat at the appointed moment in the readings, walked to the kitchen door and opened it. At that instant an astonishing event occurred. It was like nothing I had ever seen before—a thin, brilliant beam radiating pure white light, spanning from floor to ceiling. I was filled with awe. For a second I stood dazed, my mouth open, as the light moved through the doorway past me. I knew who the light was. I ran back to the table shouting, "I saw Elijah! I saw Elijah!"

My brother and my parents gaped at me.

"I just saw Elijah!" I repeated breathlessly.

They appeared numb, the three of them sitting there with their arms folded and staring at me. Finally Mom said, "Oh, Marybeth, it was just a reflection," as if that explained what I felt as well as what I had seen with my own eyes.

"A reflection of what?" I wanted to know.

"Of the kitchen light," she answered.

My father and David nodded their heads in agreement.

I argued some more, but finally my father pooh-poohed the whole thing with a wave of his arm.

I was stunned at their unwillingness to accept my explanation. I felt badly that they hadn't seen the light. I knew what I had experienced was no reflection. It was Elijah, and he had come into our home, into the very house where I lived.

Many Passovers have come and gone since, but the experience of the light has stayed with me and continues to support my spiritual

core. Eventually I combined my love of movement and music with a calling to the healing arts: I became a dance therapist, working to help those troubled by emotional conflicts find their own inner cores and open themselves up to the possibility of transformation.

Passover is about promise, the promise of God's love and light in our lives, the presence of divine power and beauty. That Passover when I was eight was an experience of grace for me. The angel Elijah blessed our home and my family and brought me a message. The vision of him was a clear indication that I would lead the spiritual life I am leading today.

Be present at our table, Lord;
Be here and everywhere adored.
These creatures bless, and grant that we
May feast in paradise with Thee.

~ John Cennick

Our Mexican Visitor

by Thelma M. Rodriguez

My husband, Eddie, and I had been together only a year and a half in 1967, but our house in Decatur, Michigan, overflowed with children. We had both been married before and there were sixteen at home besides ourselves—three of my children, ten of his, and three of his grandchildren. Eddie was in his fifties and I wasn't quite thirty. He was concerned the full house would be too much for me, but I told him not to worry. I had been raised in a big family and always imagined myself having a brood of my own someday.

But it didn't take long to realize I was overwhelmed. Raising all those children and teaching them right from wrong was tough enough, but I also had to tend to the housework. There were meals to be fixed and beds to be made. The laundry alone could take me all day. I boiled the white clothes in a galvanized tub on the stove while I put the rest in our wringer washer, and then I hung everything out to dry on the line. The chores were endless, even with some of the older kids helping. I didn't know how long I could go on this way.

Eddie worked nights driving a truck for a produce company. He was often gone for fifteen hours at a time. When he came home he had to get his sleep. I had read the Bible and prayed every night with my own children, and now I did the same with Eddie's. But no matter how hard I prayed, I just got more tired. As time passed, things didn't get any easier. I was afraid God wasn't listening to me.

Please, Lord, I begged before turning in one night, *let me know You haven't forgotten us.*

I always fixed supper around five so Eddie could sleep a few hours before he had to be back on the job at eleven. One evening about suppertime he arrived with a big Mexican man at his side. There were a lot of celery farms in Decatur in those days and some of the field-workers were Mexican. "Honey," Eddie said, "my friend needs a home till Saturday." It was nothing new for my husband to appear with a friend who needed a place to stay. They were all friends to

Eddie, even if he had just met them. I mentally added up the days and the meals I'd have to stretch while the visitor was with us. "Okay," I said.

The man was quiet, and he seemed different from the others Eddie usually brought home. Most of all, he was big—about six foot six. When he walked through our kitchen door he had to stoop. He was definitely the kind of man who stood out in a crowd.

I invited him to eat with us. "No, thank you," he responded, and then he went into the living room. Later, after Eddie had gone to bed, I was doing the dishes. Our visitor walked through the kitchen with a Bible under his arm and went outside. I watched him through the window as I finished at the sink. He sat on a wooden crate, leaning against a tree, reading in the sunset.

Every morning when I got up I always made a pot of coffee and sat down and drank a cup before I started the children's breakfast. But the first morning our visitor was there I was surprised to see my coffee already made and breakfast started. "Did you have a hard time finding everything?" I asked. He said no.

Usually, after I had breakfast going, I packed lunches and woke the kids who had to go to school. Then I fed them and helped them get dressed. After they boarded the bus I sat down and relaxed for a short time before the younger ones got up. Then I fed them and washed their faces and hands and cleaned up any mess they had made. After that I tried to eat, but the children always wanted me for something, or they started arguing and fussing and I would have to tend to them. My breakfast would be cold by the time I got back to the table.

When the children started fussing around me, our visitor said very gently, "Let Mama eat. You go play and be good." And they *were* good. It was so nice to be able to eat while my food was warm.

One day the man taught me how to make tortillas. It cost very little to fix a filling meal for all of us, and I was so grateful to him. He spoke broken English and never said much. Sometimes, if Eddie came home early, they would eat and talk awhile in Spanish. But my husband would eventually have to go to bed, and then our visitor would go out and rake the leaves in our yard. He also watched the younger children for me. They loved to play outside, but I didn't want them to be by themselves. For the first time since I could remember, I was able to do whatever I needed inside the house without having to worry about them.

Our visitor stayed till Saturday, when we took him to catch the bus. One morning soon after, Eddie came home from work strangely subdued. He kissed me and the kids and said good-bye to the ones getting ready for school. Then he headed straight for the bedroom. I thought he'd had a hard night at work and was really tired. When I went in to check on him, I found him sitting on the edge of the bed with his head in his hands.

"Honey, what's the matter?" I asked. Eddie was the type of person who would never tell me if he was sick or upset. He always kept it inside. Finally, he looked up. "Remember that big Mexican man I brought home?" he asked.

"Of course I do," I answered.

Eddie's face was pale. "Nobody else remembers him."

I sat beside Eddie as he explained. The day he met our visitor he had gotten off work early in the afternoon and stopped at a café in town for something to eat. The Mexican man walked in and went directly to Eddie's table. "May I sit down?" he said.

Eddie nodded and asked if he would like something to eat or drink. The stranger shook his head. "Why have you come to Decatur?" Eddie asked. He knew most everybody in our small town, and he'd never seen this man before.

"I've been visiting my children and thought I would stop here for a while," the stranger answered.

"Have you got a lot of children?" Eddie asked.

"Yes, quite a few," the man said.

Eddie stopped telling the story for a moment and took my hand. "The fellas thought I was drunk that afternoon," he said, "and they told me it looked like I was talking to myself. That big Mexican almost filled the doorway when he walked in, and nobody remembers him."

Later, when we asked the kids, they had no memory of him either, although he had spoken to them and they had played outside every day under his watchful eye. They got along better after his visit, almost as if he were still there telling them to be good. Things settled down in our house in general, and Eddie worried about me less. I even found time to have two cups of coffee in the morning before the kids woke up.

The Mexican man gave me a tortilla grill before he left, and I have it to this day, as a reminder of his visit. He didn't tell us much about himself, where he had come from or where he was headed. He didn't even mention his name. While he was with us, those questions seemed unimportant. But I will never forget him. He came as an answer to my prayer, because God never forgets His children.

Do not forget to entertain strangers,
for by so doing some people have
entertained angels without knowing it.

~ Hebrews 13:2

ITTLE ONES

William Wordsworth said that "Heaven lies about us in our infancy!"
Children, being so fresh to this earth, seem especially attuned to God's
messages and messengers. Eventually those precious moments of heav-
enly communication are lost to memory.

As adults we often don't really know how God is making Himself
known to our children, but occasionally a parent is privileged to glimpse
or hear about a bit of the action.

Voices in the Night

by Milagros (Milly) Trejo

By the faint glimmer of the night-light, I watched my son,
Aryel, in his crib, his chest moving in the easy rhythm of
sleep, relieved that we'd made it through another day. My husband,
Arturo, wouldn't be back from his business trip for almost a week,
and already I was exhausted from taking care of our two young children on my own.

As my gaze traced the sweep of Aryel's eyelashes and the curve of
his downy cheek, I felt a weariness not merely in my body but deep
in my soul. Asleep, my two-and-a-half-year-old seemed like any other
little boy. But when he was awake, it was painfully obvious that he
was different. He didn't interact with anyone outside our family, and
even with us, most of the time he seemed lost, locked in a world of
his own.

And according to his doctors, he would likely stay that way. I
thought back to the day a few months earlier when Arturo and I had
sat in an office at Children's Seashore House in Philadelphia, hold-

ing hands tightly, awaiting the diagnosis. A team of specialists ran a battery of hearing, psychological and neurological tests on our son. They diagnosed Aryel with a pervasive developmental disorder with autistic qualities. They said he showed some of the symptoms of autism, including speech impairment and avoidance of eye contact, yet he wasn't as emotionally unresponsive as many children with that baffling disorder.

"We are sorry to have to tell you that your son will probably never lead a normal life." The doctors' voices seemed to come from a great distance, and I could barely hear them above the clamor of questions and worries that suddenly filled my mind. *My sweet Aryel? How could it be? What went wrong?*

From the moment he came into the world, we loved him completely. Aryel had been a bright, happy baby, and he had learned to walk and talk right on schedule. At two, he toddled around the house after his sister, Aryanna, who was older by thirteen months. When he saw me he'd break into a huge smile like his dad's and say, "I love you, Mommy." He liked to point out the characters on *Sesame Street* and flip through picture books.

Then for no apparent reason, Aryel started to regress. Instead of looking at me when I spoke to him, he would stare at some point beyond me. He began losing the vocabulary he'd developed. Maybe it was only a phase. *He'll grow out of it,* I tried to tell myself. *Everything will turn out fine.* But I could not ignore the knot of anxiety that kept tightening inside me.

I asked a speech pathologist friend to take a look at him. She broke the news to me that she suspected autism, and she put me in touch with the specialists at the children's hospital. Their diagnosis shattered the illusion I'd been clinging to that everything would turn out all right.

What caused our son to develop this disorder? If there was no cure, was there at least some kind of proven treatment? Would he be able to go to school? Would he ever learn to speak again?

I desperately searched for answers, spending hours at the library and at bookstores reading up on the latest research on autism and developmental disabilities. *Why,* I wanted to know, *why our son?*

But the more I learned, the more hopeless Aryel's situation appeared. I couldn't even pray about it, not when I was looking for answers that didn't exist. No one knows the precise cause of autism or understands why some children overcome the condition while others are never able to form relationships and live independent lives.

Day by day Aryel slipped further away from us, further from the boy he had once been. No matter how much I held him, talked to him, loved him, he wanted to be alone more and more. His happy chatter died into silence. It became a constant struggle for us to figure out what he was thinking. *How can we help him if we don't know what he needs?* I kept wondering.

I repeated that question to myself as I watched Aryel sleeping quietly in his crib that night, the frustration and uncertainty of the past months threatening to devour what little strength I had left. Without Arturo there to support me, I didn't think I could go on another day. *Look at my son,* I cried out to God in my mind. *He's not even three. How could he be condemned to a world no one else understands? Please, I just want to know why!*

Finally I dragged myself away from my son's side, went to my room and collapsed into bed, falling asleep almost immediately. In the middle of the night I was awakened by a noise that sounded like people talking. I glanced at the clock. It was three in the morning. Aryanna was curled up in bed next to me, sound asleep.

The sounds were coming from the direction of Aryel's room. As I headed down the hall, I could see an intense light streaming out from under his door. It definitely wasn't the dim night-light. I pushed the door open.

My son was sitting in his crib, bathed in a brilliance I had never seen before. It was bright beyond imagination, yet strangely soothing to the eye. Aryel was looking up, rapt. I followed his gaze. The light wasn't coming from the lamps in the room or from the moon through the window. It was emanating from a being standing directly in front of him!

Even more incredible, they were having a conversation! Words came effortlessly from my son's mouth, words I couldn't decipher. Yet the being understood everything he said and responded in the same fashion.

Aryel's face wore a look of utter contentment. He must have

sensed an absolute love and acceptance flowing from this being. I felt it too.

All at once I knew what Aryel needed from us, the only thing: love and acceptance of him the way he was. Arturo and I hadn't been put in our son's life to ask why. We were there because God knew we could help him. The fears and worries and questions that had tormented me for months were swept away in that brilliant luminescence, and I knew I must be experiencing the same peace that glowed on my son's face, God's peace.

See that you do not look down on one of these little ones. For I tell you that their angels in heaven always see the face of my Father in heaven.

~ Matthew 18:10

Hanna's Pretties

by Ava Chambers

My youngest, Hanna, and I are a close-knit pair. Maybe it's because she was born on my birthday, or maybe it's because she nearly died so young. She was a healthy newborn but soon grew sickly and was finally diagnosed with a severe respiratory condition. At twelve months she had to be hospitalized. The diagnosis was grim. Hanna slipped into a coma. It was a difficult time for us all. My husband, Russell, was a rock of strength, and so were my parents, especially my dad, to whom I was also especially close.

After five days Hanna miraculously woke up. The day she was discharged her big green eyes took a final look around her room. "Bye-bye, pretties," she said, waving her tiny hands. At least I *thought* that's what she said.

I was so overjoyed to have Hanna home, to hear her sweet voice while she played. I had missed her chatter. Sitting on the floor in her room, her doll baby propped up next to her, Hanna formed a few words into what sounded like a question. I heard the word *pretties*. She waited in silence for several seconds, then responded as if she were having a conversation. Her older sisters, Rebecca and Sara, had had imaginary friends too, but they didn't have conversations with them. Hanna's pretties were different. She seemed to think they talked back. *What an imagination!* I marveled.

As Hanna got older she couldn't understand why the rest of the world didn't see their own pretties. Sometimes she offered to lend us hers. One early December I received a catalog filled with Christmas decorations and gifts. On the back cover was a picture of an angel figurine, her sweeping wings spanning the width of the page.

Hanna pointed to the picture and squealed. "My pretties! My pretties!"

"We call those angels," I explained.

"An—gel," Hanna repeated slowly. I could see her processing the connection in her head. But did I believe Hanna's imaginary friends were really angels?

Soon after, my life was thrown into turmoil when both my mother and father contracted pneumonia and were admitted to the hospital. All day I bounced from Mom's room to Dad's in the intensive care unit. But I stayed longer with Dad. His emphysema hampered his ability to fight off illness.

In the evenings I made the hundred-mile trip from the hospital back to my own home, in Acworth, Georgia. After a week my father's condition worsened, and one night I decided to stay over at the hospital. I dreaded telling the children I wasn't coming home, especially Hanna. She was only three and had never spent a night without her mama.

Tears welled up in my eyes as I dialed the number. Hanna answered. "I love you, Mommy," she bubbled. "I want to tell you something! Know what?"

I tried to compose myself. "What, sugar? What do you want to tell Mommy?"

"My angels said they were coming to get Papa, but not till church day."

I was speechless. I hung up quickly, but her words stuck with me.

The next day I found my daddy sitting up in bed having his eggs and coffee. He smiled, in good spirits. "Hi, Princess," he said. Dad used to call me that when I was a little girl. It always made me feel good to hear it. I was adopted and Daddy said he picked me out special. For the first five years of my life, I thought Princess was my real name.

That afternoon, Saturday, I set up a "date" for my parents to have in the hospital. Mama fluffed up her hair and a nurse donated some lipstick. I helped her into a wheelchair and brought her to Dad's room. They held hands and talked for almost an hour. *God,* I prayed, *help them heal so they can come home soon.*

That evening I went back home for dinner. As we were eating, Hanna repeated what her angels had told her. *That child's imagination!* I thought, dismissing her reminder. For the first time in many days I felt hope that my parents would soon get better.

After baths and story time, Russell and I tucked the kids in. Hanna begged to sleep with me and I relented. In the middle of the night I awoke with a start. Unable to go back to sleep, I eased away from

Hanna's embrace. I walked down the hall to get a drink of water. The silence was pierced by the ringing phone.

It can't be good news, I thought, picking up the receiver. The ICU nurse urged me to come immediately. Daddy had taken a turn for the worse. I raced to the hospital. In the ICU I held his hand. *I can't lose my daddy. I can't, Lord.*

My father passed away at 7:00 A.M., just as the first rays of the sun shone through the unit's window. Sunday morning. Church day. I remembered Hanna's words. Had the angels come for Daddy?

At the funeral Hanna stood close by my side in the receiving line. Over and over she heard mourners say to me, "I'm sorry for your loss." Finally she blurted, "My Papa is not lost! My angels took him. You should all be happy!" Grand words from a three-year-old, I admit.

I bent down and gave Hanna a hug. "Thank you, honey." I knew folks would think Hanna was just mimicking adults, repeating what they assumed she had overheard. But I knew better.

ANGELS ON THE

MOUNTAIN

Mountaintops have come to represent exhilarating high points in life. But the steep path to or from a summit is treacherous for hikers, bikers, drivers . . . anyone on the move. In a frightful ride down a Tennessee mountain, Allan Traphagan learned a lesson about "the way God works in the world": that "He is with us all the time."

The psalmist knew this also, using a mountain metaphor to make the point that "the Lord surrounds his people" just "as the mountains surround Jerusalem" (Psalm 125:2).

Riding Down Signal Mountain

by Allan W. Traphagan

As a young man Dad rode his bicycle to work. Just like him, I used to bike to my job at a citrus factory in Florida. I was in good shape in June, about twenty years ago, when I decided to make a long-distance bike trip to see my dad, who was slowly dying of cancer back home in South Bend, Indiana.

Some co-workers thought about coming along on the fifteen-hundred-mile trek, but one by one they chickened out. It was just me and my Lotus ten-speed.

In the heat I wore a sweatshirt with the sleeves cut off, and Levis to protect my legs from rocks and rattlesnakes. My backpack held a change of clothes and a bottle of water. I usually started around 4:00 A.M. and rode till sundown, eating in coffee shops and sleeping in back-road motels.

Florida's heavy traffic and Georgia's mountainous roads slowed me down. I'd been traveling eight days when I finally crossed into Tennessee and reached the top of Signal Mountain outside Chattanooga, about halfway home. The air was cool up there, so I decided to rest for a while. I got off my bike and took in the view.

Houses were scattered among the trees below me. A bearded man waved from his porch. *He looks like Dad,* I thought, and turned my gaze north, toward Indiana. Picturing my father sitting on his own front porch, I said angrily, "It's not fair you're suffering." He'd always had faith in a loving God who watched over us. *Kid stuff.* I'd learned to do things for myself. I'd decided God left us alone, at least in this world. It seemed especially true to me now. God sure wasn't taking care of my dad.

I jumped on my bike and pedaled back to the road. The black asphalt wound downward. I looked up at the mountaintop, admiring its crown of stately trees against the misty clouds. Gaining speed, I rounded a bend and was caught off-guard by the narrow road ahead. It plunged straight down the mountain. *I'm going too fast!* I tightened my grip on the handlebars, testing the front and back brakes, trying to stay near the center of the road. On my right was a wall of rock; on my left a sheer drop.

I applied the brakes a little harder. If I pressed them all the way at this speed, I'd flip over the handlebars. But the bike wasn't slowing down enough, and I was going too fast to jump off. I squeezed the levers tighter as I sped around a curve. Then I smelled smoke. *The brakes! They'll burn up!* I glued my eyes to the road. Nothing would stop me if I careened off the side; I'd fall to the rocky ledges below.

I tightened the brakes, but the smell of smoke was so strong I knew they were nearly gone. Another sharp curve came up before me, and I wobbled close to the edge of the cliff.

As I fought to keep steady, I heard a frightening roar. Then I was struck hard from behind. Looking back quickly I saw the giant chrome grille and bumper of a truck! I hadn't even heard it approaching. The force of the bump propelled my bike down the mountain faster than ever. I glanced around again. I could see the driver's face through the windshield. He was nodding, half asleep. *He doesn't know I'm in front of him!*

I nearly closed my eyes, dreading the terrible impact. Then suddenly I saw them: tall, muscular men, each one different but all with massive white wings. Dozens of them, airborne, sailing down the mountain with me, floating over the valley below. *Angels?*

"Help me!" I screamed. But they didn't seem to hear. They were laughing and talking to each other. Somehow the distraction steadied me. I relaxed a little and regained control of my bike.

Ahead of me lay a boulder the size of a washtub. I swerved around it almost effortlessly. From behind I heard air brakes hissing like a great dragon. Then screeching and crunching sounds. At this speed I didn't dare look back.

I heard a massive scrape and then nothing—just the wind singing in my ears as I continued down the mountain. The angels had disappeared. Finally, the last steep descent led me onto a long, flat road into the Sequatchie Valley.

I coasted to a country store. The clerk called the police, and I waited till we learned that the truck driver was all right. I was shaking so hard I couldn't get back on my bike, so I pushed it till I found a motel for the night.

When I reached home more than seven hundred miles later, my father said he'd been worried about me. "I had help along the way," I said.

"From the looks of you," he replied, "you must have."

It wasn't my leathery, tanned skin or wind-whipped hair or the weight I'd lost. It must have been something in my eyes. I could still picture clearly those laughing angels. The sight of them had kept me steady. Their joy had kept me alive.

Dad and I had a long talk. I described what had happened high atop Signal Mountain, and how it had changed my mind about the way God works in the world. "Now I see," I said. "He is with us all the time."

Dad surprised me. "I've had my own doubts lately," he confessed. "I've wondered if God is truly aware of what I'm going through with this illness. 'Where are You when I really need You?' I've asked. I guess you've shown me, Son. He's here, as always."

His angels had convinced both my father and me that whatever road we're traveling, we're not traveling alone.

Storm on the Mountain

by Shirley Braverman

Through the swirling snowfall in the San Jacinto Mountains of California, I could see Ray the forest ranger on the road in front of me. I was so angry and in such a hurry to get to my cabin, I was tempted to ignore him when he flagged me down.

I pumped the brake and brought my truck, Betsy, to a stop. "Look, Ray," I said through clenched teeth, "please don't tell me I can't go through. I only live a mile and a half up the mountain, and I'm not exactly inexperienced at driving in the snow."

He frowned. I could see his nose was almost frozen. "I don't have any authority to turn back residents," he said, "but it's been coming down hard for three hours now. You can hardly see. And there could be an avalanche anytime."

"I'll drive slow," I promised and went on my way.

In the past I'd driven home in torrential rain, pounding hail, icy sleet, and through clouds that crept up the mountain and sat down on the road as if they owned it. But I had to admit this blinding snowstorm was some of the worst weather I'd seen. I hunched over the wheel, focusing on the road. Not that the road got all my attention. I was hot with anger at my daughter-in-law.

My husband, daughter and son had been killed in an accident on a Los Angeles freeway less than three years before, and not a day had gone by when I didn't struggle through all the feelings that still tormented me in the aftermath of that tragedy. My cabin in the San Jacinto Mountains was my only refuge from the harsh realities of life. My son's wife, crazy with grief, had taken up with a brute of a man. I told her he wasn't right for the kids. I told her to leave him, but she ignored me. She'd finally left him and now, after all this time, she wanted my help. Wanted to move in with me so she could go back to school. With me, in my tiny mountain cabin! We'd had a terrible fight back at her apartment in the city. The kids had cried and I'd stormed out.

I squinted into the whirling snow. *I need my peace and quiet. I deserve it,* I thought. But I knew the real reason I didn't want to help. I no longer had the heart; whatever love I'd had to give had died with my family.

It was getting harder to see out the windshield. This was exactly why Ray didn't want to let me up here. But I was stubborn, set in my ways. I knew it. When my daughter-in-law had called me stubborn, however, I had accused her of being insensitive.

I banged the flat of my hand on the steering wheel. I couldn't see anything. Nothing but darkness ahead. Like my future.

If only things could be different, I thought. *If only I could start over again without all this anger and hurt in my soul.* I held the wheel tight with both hands, peering into the darkness.

Then, suddenly a sunlit patch opened up before me. A column of snow seemed to dance in front of my car. I gasped and hit the brake. There in the center of the column was the image of an old woman. She looked like my dear grandmother, who'd nurtured me as a child. She had cared for me when my parents went to work in a factory during World War II, and had saved her money all year to buy me a wonderful Christmas dress. The vision held out a hand as if in warning.

"Go back!" she said. "Go back!"

Had I really heard the words through the moaning of the storm, or were they just in my head? I blinked and looked again. The sunlight was still there, but the image of the woman was gone.

I could feel the tears streaming down my face, the beating of my heart within my breast. I felt as I had as a child, surrounded and nourished by my grandmother's love. Love I had thought I would never feel again. Love I should be passing on . . .

To my left was the only turnout on the road. I threw my truck into gear, turned around and headed down the mountain the way I'd come.

When I got back to the ranger station, Ray ran out to meet me. "Thank God you're okay!" he yelled. "An avalanche hit minutes after you left. The spotters called it in on the radio. It took out the road above the turnout.

"You're welcome to spend the night with my wife and me," Ray offered. "Might be a few days before the road is cleared."

"That's very kind of you," I said awkwardly, "but I've got to go down to the city again. My grandkids and their mother need me." He waved me on.

When my grandmother lay ailing at the end of her life, I had been heartbroken at the thought of never seeing her again. She'd promised me that when she got to heaven she would make sure I was always watched over. On a snowy mountain road God had sent an angel I could not fail to recognize to redirect my life. I had a new reason for living: to be the grandmother that my grandmother had been to me, to share the love she had shared with me. I gunned the truck and said, "Come on, Betsy, I have family waiting."

Father, Who has made the mountains . . .
Hear Your children's morning prayer,
Asking for Your guardian care;
Keep and guide us all the day,
Lead us safely all the way.

~ Frances Ridley Havergal

URSERY

"Sleep in heavenly peace." That's what Joseph Mohr wrote of the infant Jesus. But it's also what mothers and fathers everywhere can request for the babies they are welcoming into the world. With faith, we can ask that God send His angels to keep a special watch over the innocent, vulnerable babies given to our care.

Stranger on Our Doorstep

by Arthur A. Best

The old country doctor set his black bag on the bedside table. "I'm sorry, ma'am," he said. "I'm afraid your boy isn't going to make it through the night. A blue baby, and a month and a half premature, at that . . ." His words trailed off.

Exhausted from the difficult birth, Garnet nodded and leaned back against her pillows. Compared to her older sons and daughter, who had been sturdy newborns, this baby looked frail and helpless. Garnet knew the boy's chances were slim at best. Besides, if an emergency arose, she and her husband, Elmer, wouldn't be able to get medical help fast enough, living as they did up a hollow several miles from the nearest town. Their farm lay along a creek, and the only way coming or going was a dusty dirt road.

The doctor cleared his throat. "I have to take your baby with me," he said. "The next twenty-four hours are critical. If he makes it, I'll

bring him back tomorrow afternoon." The doctor picked up the baby and carefully settled him inside the black medical bag.

Garnet bit her lip, watching her boy being swallowed up by the worn leather satchel, tiny as he was. "Thank you, Doctor," she said, the softness of her voice matching the quiet of that spring day in 1933. "We're grateful."

Elmer saw the doctor to the door then returned to his wife's bedside. "Doc will take good care of him," he told her. He held her hand, his work-roughened fingers gently curling around hers. "All we can do is pray."

"I know," she whispered, her eyes half closed. "I already am . . ." She drifted off to sleep.

The next day the whole family—Garnet, Elmer and their three older children—anxiously awaited the good doctor's arrival. Garnet napped fitfully, her thoughts constantly returning to her sickly baby. When a knock finally came at the door, Elmer ran to open it.

"Your boy survived the night," the doctor said, "although I can't quite say how." He lifted the baby out of his bag and placed the tiny bundle in Garnet's arms. The boy still looked alarmingly small, but at least he had a little color.

"Get some milk in him," the doctor instructed. "And keep him warm. He seems to be allergic to cow's milk, but you shouldn't have any trouble if you nurse him." Garnet nodded, feeling reassured.

Not long after the doctor left, the baby awakened with a weak mew. "Are you hungry?" Garnet murmured, and she began to nurse him. She was glad to see he had a healthy appetite.

He drank his fill and nodded off, seemingly content. But before long, he began to bawl. "What's the matter, little one?" Garnet asked, gently rubbing his back. The baby promptly spit up nearly all he had consumed. *Maybe he drank too fast,* she thought. *I'll make sure he takes it slower next time.*

The next time—in fact, every time—she nursed him, however, produced the same dreadful results. By nightfall, she was desperate. "He's never going to get stronger if he can't hold his milk down," she told her husband. Remembering the doctor's admonition to keep the baby warm, she put him in a woven basket, blanket and all, and slipped him under the toasty cookstove.

The following day brought no change in the baby. Garnet continued to feed him, hoping he'd keep enough in his stomach for nourishment. By late afternoon he was whimpering constantly, whether from hunger or from illness, Garnet couldn't tell. She and her husband agreed: It was time to find the doctor.

As Elmer laced up his boots, a faint knock came at the door. Had the doctor decided to stop by? Eagerly Elmer flung the door open. "Doc, we were just—" He stopped short, surprised, when he saw the stranger standing there.

Unfamiliar people had stopped on their doorstep before. During those hard times, folks were walking around everywhere, looking for work in exchange for a hot meal and a place to sleep. But this woman was different. She was black. In this area of southeastern Ohio, there were very few black people, and they always kept to themselves.

"Do you think you could let me have something to eat," she asked, "and maybe a place to stay? It'll only be until I get my strength back. I had a baby yesterday, and I'm just too tired to go on." When she saw the question in Elmer's expression, she added, "My child was stillborn."

"I'm sorry," Elmer replied, beckoning her in. He led her to the rocking chair in front of the stove, where his wife sat trying to soothe the baby. "I'm Elmer Best, and this is my wife, Garnet. Garnet, this is . . ."

"Jane. Just call me Jane," the woman said. "I promise I'll earn my keep."

"Now I've got to fetch the doctor," Elmer said. "My wife will show you where you can stay." He hurried out, and Garnet explained the situation with the baby.

"I can see you have your hands full," Jane said, gazing sympathetically at the boy in Garnet's arms. "Let me get supper on." While Garnet sat in the rocking chair, desperately trying to quiet her newborn, Jane slowly and methodically fixed a pot of soup from beef bones and vegetables.

By the time Elmer returned, the children had all been fed. "Doc's over in the next county on an emergency," he said, crestfallen. "He won't be back until tomorrow at the earliest."

"Don't worry," Jane said. "I have a feeling your boy will be all right."

After settling the baby in for the night, in his makeshift cradle under the stove, Garnet went to sleep, prayers swirling in her mind. *Lord, please help our child,* she pleaded. *Show us what he needs.*

She awoke feeling more hopeful. When she peeked in the basket to say good morning to their boy, it was empty. In a panic, she yelled for her husband. Their baby wasn't any place in sight. Neither was Jane.

"I'm going to check the property," Elmer said, trying to stay calm.

Garnet waited and paced by the stove. Why had they helped this woman? What if she'd run away with their baby? Finally Garnet heard her husband calling from the distance, "I found them!" She raced to the door, relieved to see Elmer with the baby.

"I found them in one of the outbuildings," he explained. "She was letting him nurse from her and hid because she wasn't sure how we would react."

Garnet took her son in her arms and held him close. "Look, Elmer," she said slowly, "her milk seems to agree with him." It was true: The baby was sleeping peacefully, no crying, no spitting up.

Elmer went to get Jane. After she returned to the house, the three of them agreed on the arrangement and didn't speak of the incident again. Nor did they discuss when Jane would leave. Instead she became, in a way, part of the family.

Soon Elmer was back on the job cutting timber, and the two women were busy running the household. Jane never talked much, especially about herself, and Garnet wasn't one to pry. The infant grew slowly but steadily.

One morning Garnet and Elmer arose, expecting Jane's good morning at breakfast as usual. When she wasn't at the stove, Elmer went to see if she was ill. But her bed hadn't been slept in, and her few possessions were nowhere to be found. She wasn't in the garden or anywhere else on their property.

Elmer rushed to their neighbors' place down the creek and asked if they'd seen her. No one had. Not so much as a dog had barked to announce someone passing. He got to thinking, *Did anyone even see her when she came to us?*

When he asked, the neighbors looked bewildered. A black woman wandering these parts would have been noticed, they assured him. The folks at the other farms Jane would have passed on the dirt road to their house didn't know what Elmer was talking about either.

In the months that followed, he and Garnet even asked friends in other counties if they had seen a woman fitting Jane's description. The answer was always no. It was as if the earth gave birth to her and when she left, the earth swallowed her up again.

Garnet and Elmer were practical folk, with their feet firmly planted on the ground, and they didn't spend a lot of time pondering the mystery of Jane's visit. But whenever they spoke of her, their eyes filled with wonder. I should know. I was that sickly baby boy, and I often heard the story of how a stranger arrived from nowhere to give me the nourishment that only she could give.

Mission for Mikey

by Mabel Grayson*

y oldest daughter, April, was a sweet girl. Innocent and vivacious, she enjoyed playing mommy to her younger brothers and sister. Working with the Special Olympics was her passion. I had never seen a teenager with more patience and with such an affinity for kids. From the time April was little, she dreamed of raising a family of her own.

But when she grew up and got married, she became less and less like the April I knew. She stopped seeing her old friends. Her behavior became irresponsible, her answers evasive. It didn't take long for me to realize she was on drugs. It turned out that her husband had been an addict before she was. Saddest of all, when she finally had the children she had always wanted, three of them, she wasn't in any shape to be a mother. There were times when I could see that she really loved those kids. But they needed to be loved *all* the time, and drugs ruled April's life.

Often, she dropped off the children at my place, promising to return in a couple of hours, which became days, even weeks. April would simply vanish, running, I learned later, from her abusive husband. Finally she just handed over my three grandchildren. I was relieved that I could protect them and keep them together as a family. We saw little of April, and finally nothing at all.

One winter Saturday, I was running errands with three-year-old Mikey, when he made a strange announcement: "We have a new brother," he said from the backseat.

"What are you talking about?"

Mikey stood up behind me. "He was born today, Grandma. We have to go find him."

Blond, blue-eyed Mikey was as mischievous and unpredictable as any three-year-old, but he had never come up with an odd statement

*Name has been changed.

like this one. Another grandchild? *Born Saturday, January 25, 1992,* I noted.

Then I caught myself. *Surely Mikey is making this up.* Lord only knew what went through Mikey's mind, with parents who had dropped out of his life. When we had last seen April, six months before, she hadn't looked pregnant. Since then I had tried to track her down; I called her friends and visited her hangouts. Nobody had said anything to me about April being pregnant. And surely Mikey had not heard from her.

"Mikey," I said as we pulled into our driveway, "you have one brother and one sister, and you three kids live with me. You're all together, safe. Grandma's going to take care of you." Helping him out of the car, I saw he was thinking hard.

That winter Saturday was a sunny and warm southern California day. A neighbor child ran over to play with Mikey in our front yard. *Maybe he'll get his mind off this foolishness,* I thought. I spread out my sewing on the living room table and opened the French doors so I could keep an eye on the children.

I didn't pay much attention to their conversation until I heard Mikey say it was his new brother's birthday. Exasperated, I called my grandson inside. "Mikey, how on earth did you come up with such a story?"

Silently he studied me. "Well?" I demanded.

Mikey huffed, "The angel told me so."

"Told you what?" I asked. "When?"

"An angel and Jesus came to me when I was asleep last night, Grandma, and the angel said I have a new brother. We have to go find him!" Mikey was so adamant, I found myself almost believing him. *But since when do angels bring important messages to three-year-olds?*

"What did Jesus look like?" I asked, testing.

"He was all shiny. I couldn't see His face because it was too bright."

"And the angel, Mikey? What did the angel look like?"

My grandson smiled and ran his hands down the length of his outfit. "All white," he said. "And big and shining!" Then he ran back outside to play, leaving me to sort it all out. Now, more than ever, I wished I could find April, if only to set my mind at ease that I had all her children safe in my care. *Lord,* I asked, *if there was an angel, why didn't You let me see it?* I mulled this over until one of the children needed my attention; to tell the truth, with the constant activity, I didn't have much trouble putting the whole mysterious episode out of my mind.

Four days later we received an unexpected bill from the hospital. *What's this about?* I wondered, ripping open the envelope. None of us had been sick. When I unfolded the invoice, I couldn't believe my eyes. "Patient: April Franklin," it read in bold letters. And then, "Ultrasound." As far as I knew, there was only one reason for a young woman to get an ultrasound reading. And then I remembered Mikey's dream.

Perhaps this was all one big mix-up. What were the odds of April being pregnant again—and Mikey knowing about it without having had any word from her? I decided to call the hospital and find out.

"Is April Franklin your patient?" I asked the operator. She checked the list and said no. Another dead end. I started to hang up when I remembered Mikey's urgent request to find his new brother. "This is an emergency," I blurted out. "I must speak to Admissions."

On hold, I listened to droning Muzak. Was I on a wild-goose chase? All because of a little boy's dream?

"Admissions," said the woman on the other end. "April Franklin was discharged."

"I am her mother," I said quickly. "Do you know how to reach her?"

There was an uncomfortable pause on the other end. "She was brought in from the county jail," the woman explained. "I assume she has been taken back there."

I hung up brokenhearted. Part of me didn't want to know what had happened. But I could not shake the feeling that Mikey knew something important.

I took a deep breath and looked up the number for the county jail. How many times had I dialed the telephone, dreading what I was going to learn about April?

"County jail," a gruff voice answered. I explained who I was, and finally the matron came to the phone with some answers. I found out that April had been arrested for failure to pay fines on innumerable parking and traffic violations. "Is my daughter all right?" I interrupted. "Is she . . . pregnant?"

"April's baby was born prematurely."

I caught my breath. *Born?* "Where is he?" I asked, realizing I had assumed the baby was a boy, just as Mikey had predicted.

"I'm sorry," the matron said. "I'm not allowed to give out that information."

"I have custody of April's other children," I said, keeping my voice steady, "and I don't want this one to fall into the system."

There was silence on the other end. Finally she said, "If I were you, and no one was allowed to tell me the whereabouts of a premature baby, I would start at the county hospital."

I couldn't keep the smile off my face. "Thank you for the advice," I said.

Driving my car, I needed every ounce of self-restraint I could muster to stay within the speed limit. Still, I wasn't sure what to expect. Had April really brought another child into this world? *If she has, God, what do you want me to do? Can I handle one more under my roof? I'm not sure I can love another baby.*

I flew into the hospital and into the neonatal ward. "I've come to see the Franklin baby," I said, not fully believing the words coming out of my own mouth. "I'm the grandmother."

"I'm so glad you've come," the nurse said. "The baby's kidney infection is clearing up and he's due to be released to . . ." As we walked, she checked the chart and read the name of one of April's friends. I had arrived in the nick of time!

The nurse led me through a maze of incubators and stopped in front of one. "Here we are," she said pleasantly. Inside lay a tiny but perfectly formed little boy. Mikey had been right after all. He had a new brother. A precious miracle, just as each of April's other children had been. "When was he born?" I asked the nurse, although by now I knew.

"Last Saturday," she said. "January 25. He came early."

I asked the nurse the name of my new grandson. She smiled and said, "I'm not sure. We just call him Baby Angel."

I immediately fell in love with his tight, pink face, his eyes not quite open. His arms and legs moved herky-jerky, and he seemed to stick his chest out, saying, "Look at me, Grandma." *There's plenty of love left in my heart for you, little one.*

It was hard to tear myself away from him, but I had no time to waste. "I'll be back," I whispered.

From the lobby, I called our lawyer and asked him to seek immediate custody. "I'll do what I can," he promised. In less than twenty-four hours, he was able to get an injunction against giving the baby to April's friend, who had a police record for drug possession. The child would be put under my protection upon release from the hospital.

Now I had to go see April. I waited for her in the visitors' room at the county jail. When she walked in, I could see that she was furious. She said she had done everything she could to keep the baby a secret because she was determined to raise him herself. "I want my children!" she said through clenched teeth. "And I'll keep having babies until I get to keep one!"

"You should know by now how much God loves you and your children," I answered quietly. "If you keep having them, He'll keep taking them away—using angels if necessary—until you quit using drugs." Then I told her about Mikey's prophetic dream.

April cut our visit short. She seemed truly touched by what I had told her.

When we brought the new baby home, Mikey fell easily into his role of big brother. Of course, he had already fulfilled his mission: He had heeded the angel's message.

We didn't hear from April for a long time. When she finally called, it was from a rehabilitation clinic. She had been off drugs for three months and was separating from her husband. "I'm going to make it this time, Mom," she said. She sounded different; she sounded like April.

Later, when I saw her, she said the words I never thought I would hear: "I thank God every day for a mother like you. I want to show my children that I love them as much as you love me."

OVERSEAS

"In Christ there is no East or West," wrote poet John Oxenham long be-fore there was an Iron Curtain, a Bamboo Curtain, a Berlin Wall. The following stories are played out in the context of the world's "East-West" political divisions after World War II. They well show that no matter where we live or where we travel, God is there—on both sides of great walls intended to keep one group of people separated from another.

China Crossing

by Joseph Celona

fter years of drifting from place to place, searching for some sense of purpose, I ended up on a deserted Maui beach one night in 1986, feeling more lost than ever. "God, who am I? How do I find my way?" I gazed up at the sky as if the answer were written in the stars. "How do I find You?"

I heard a voice, gentle yet firm, coming not from outside myself, but from inside. *Go to church.* Church? I had given that up years ago. But I'd tried everything else, so that Sunday I went and sat in the back pew of a small chapel. I could slip out if I didn't like it.

Amazingly, the sermon seemed to be directed at me. "Jesus wants you just as you are," the minister declared. "He'll set you on your feet again." The next thing I knew, I was walking up to the altar. "I give myself to You," I promised God. "Please lead me where You want me to go."

Not long after, an opening came up on the staff of Youth with a Mission, YWAM. It was the direction I'd been seeking for my life, I was sure! Though I was a little disappointed to be assigned to mun-

dane janitorial duty, I threw myself into my job, and, even more, into studying the Bible. I wanted a complete understanding of every aspect of my faith. That way doubts couldn't creep in and stall me as they had in the past.

The biblical book that fascinated me most was Acts, the stories of Jesus' disciples crisscrossing the Mediterranean to spread His Word—maybe because I wanted to do missionary work myself. I couldn't get the images out of my mind. An angel opening the prison doors and escorting the apostles out to the temple in Jerusalem. Another angel in Antioch loosening the chains that bound Peter between two soldiers and leading him right past the guards undetected. An earthquake shaking a Macedonian jail to its foundations and freeing Paul and Silas from their shackles. It all seemed so wild—and at the same time, so real!

But the more I read, the more I questioned. Did the present day measure up to biblical times? Did these kinds of things happen anymore? Although Christians were still imprisoned for their beliefs—for instance, in China, where the government cracked down on pretty much any form of worship—I had yet to hear of angels coming to their aid. I felt the wonder of my newfound faith starting to fade.

Then one day a supervisor took me aside. "We need someone to smuggle a thousand Bibles into China," he said. "It'll be dangerous, but people there have no other way of getting them. Think you're up to it?"

"Of course!" Now this was the kind of work I had imagined myself doing for God, a mission that would make my faith exciting again.

I was briefed down to the last detail. I would be teamed with a more experienced smuggler, another guy who worked for YWAM. We were to rendezvous in the British colony of Hong Kong, then travel by train to mainland China.

"There aren't any X-ray machines at the Shenzhen border crossing," my supervisor told me. "The inspectors won't find anything unless they hand-search, and they won't bother as long as you don't look suspicious." After we made it across the border, Chinese pastors would switch bags with us, taking the Bibles to distribute in their underground churches.

I flew to Hong Kong, suitcases laden with pocket-sized Bibles. My anticipation mounting, I stepped into bustling Kowloon Tong railway station, our designated meeting spot. Though I'd never met my partner (I had been given only his description), I spotted him right away by the ticket window. It wasn't hard to pick out the tall, skinny American amid the Chinese people hurrying to catch their trains.

We'd been instructed to do everything we could to avoid drawing attention to ourselves. So instead of chatting, we just nodded hello, then went upstairs to the platform, lugging our precious cargo.

A silver train glided to a stop, and the doors slid open in front of us. We settled into our seats, our suitcases by our feet, where we could keep an eye on them. As we left the station, my partner opened a paperback. I looked out the window. The emerald hills and rice paddies we passed seemed a world away from the mirrored skyscrapers of Hong Kong.

Forty-five minutes later our train pulled into Lo Wu station, the entry point for Shenzhen. With the other passengers, we headed for the customs and immigration area. Remembering my supervisor's warning, I glanced at my partner, weighed down by his bags. *If I look as jittery as he does,* I worried, *we'll be in handcuffs within minutes.*

Soldiers with machine guns were posted around the perimeter. *Stay calm,* I told myself. My companion's face paled. I followed his gaze. Something more frightening stood at the far end of the room— a battery of X-ray inspection units!

"We're finished," my partner whispered. "We'll have to turn back."

I was too tense even to nod. Then I thought of the Chinese pastors and their congregations. They risked their lives every day to do what we took for granted. *We want to help these people, God,* I prayed, *but You've got to tell us how.*

I looked around the room frantically. Did we have any other options? To the right of the X-ray machines was the exit corridor from mainland China. A phalanx of armed guards kept close watch over those coming through it, Chinese citizens who wanted to visit Hong Kong.

Go through that corridor. Walk backward.

I recognized that voice! The same interior voice had urged me to

go to church that lonely night months earlier—exactly the advice I'd needed then. But what was this now? Enter through the *exit* corridor? Walk *backward?* The only Americans in a roomful of Chinese people, we already stood out. Why risk drawing any more attention to ourselves? It didn't make sense. But I whispered the instructions to my partner anyway.

"We'll be shot!" he said.

"Trust me, we've got to do it this way," I insisted, trying to quell my doubts as well as his. There was no time to argue.

The crowd pushed us up to the customs declaration table. I shakily filled out the form. At the window, the immigration officer checked my passport and visa, then waved me toward the X-ray machines—and definite disaster.

I took a deep breath and made for the exit corridor. *God, it's tough to follow You when I don't understand Your plan, but I don't have a choice here.* I turned around to face the room. With a single hesitant step, I moved backward into the hallway. I took another step, then another.

Mutters of protest went up as I walked into the people who were going in the right direction, heading out. I could only pray the guards couldn't hear the commotion. My heavy suitcases bumped an elderly woman in the knees. "Sorry," I whispered, stumbling. She clucked at me disapprovingly.

I fought through the crowd. It was hard, like trying to do the backstroke upstream. Sweat dripped down my neck. I kept checking over my shoulder so I wouldn't crash into anyone, but it didn't help much. I was going the wrong way, after all.

As I neared the mouth of the corridor, a guard strode forward, gun at the ready, combat boots thudding on the floor. He said something in rapid-fire Chinese, then paused ten feet from me and scanned the crowd. I didn't dare peer over my shoulder, but I could feel his eyes raking over me.

Still walking backward, I inched closer to the end of the hall. The guard didn't stop me. When I pulled even with him, he looked right at me. But he didn't react at all. Not a flicker of expression crossed his face. I might as well have been cloaked in some magical veil. His gaze bored not into me but *through* me. How was this possible?

Then I saw my partner. He'd followed my instructions. Awkwardly, he backed toward me, worriedly glancing at the soldiers. But they looked past him too. Although everyone else could see us, to all the guards we were invisible!

Moments later I emerged from the corridor. I'd made it! I was safely across the border in Shenzhen, China. I turned and faced forward again. There was a wooden bench in front of me. I collapsed onto it to wait for my partner, feeling as if I'd just stepped from the pages of one of the Bibles I was smuggling.

Maybe I didn't see the angel who draped us in her wondrous veil. Maybe I didn't fully understand the power that had rendered us invisible. But there was no question that my partner and I had been shielded from the guards and led right past them. Kind of like the apostles I'd read so much about in Acts. And like them, I had been set free. Free from the doubts that had always plagued me. Free to follow God's direction. Free, at last, to truly believe.

My Russian Soldier

by Renie Szilak Burghardt

*T*he first time I laid eyes on my Russian guardian angel, he was pointing a machine gun at me and my grandparents. It was the spring of 1945. The Soviet Army was sweeping through my homeland of Hungary, driving out the Nazi troops, but committing their own atrocities. My grandparents and I had traveled for months in our horse-drawn wagon, seeking refuge from the new oppressors. By day we'd move swiftly, ready to jump out and take cover in a ditch if bombs began falling. At night we camped with other refugees. I lay in my feather bed in the back of the wagon holding Paprika, the old orange tabby cat that had belonged to my mother, who died when I was just a baby. War was almost all I had known during my seven years. There seemed to be no place that was safe. I tried to remember the face of my mother and of my father, who had gone away to fight a couple of years earlier, but I could only picture people I had seen killed when the shells had come too close.

We finally settled in a house in a rural area, and Grandpa and some other men built a bunker. We had just spent a sleepless night there, while the warplanes buzzed overhead and the bombs thundered around us. Then all at once it became quiet. Cautiously we crept out into the soft darkness of early dawn and headed back to our house. The brush crackled under our feet as my grandparents and I walked past a small cemetery. The markers looked lonely, each one separated from the others by tall weeds. I shivered.

Suddenly there was a rustle in the bushes just ahead. Two men jumped out and pointed machine guns at us.

"*Stoi!*" one of the men shouted. Paprika leaped out of my arms.

"Russians!" my grandfather whispered. "Stand still and—"

But I was already running after my cat. I darted between the soldiers and scooped her up. The younger of the two soldiers, a tall, dark-haired man, approached me. I cringed, holding Paprika against my chest like a shield. He reached out and petted her. "I have a little girl about your age back in Russia, and she has a cat just like this," he said, gently tugging one of my blonde braids. I looked up into his kind brown eyes and smiled.

We were told that Hungary was now mostly under Soviet control. But the younger soldier, who said his name was Ivan, assured us we would not be harmed. "Maybe you'd like some food," Grandma offered. The soldiers came to the house and ate breakfast with us, meager as it was.

Ivan returned the next day with a can of sardines. "For Paprika," he said. He stayed for dinner and told us about his home and family. From then on, he came by at least once a week to eat Grandma's cooking and bring me little treats.

"My own daughter is far away, *malka*," he would say, "but at least I have you to spoil." I loved his visits, yet I was terrified of the Russians in general. We had heard rumors of Hungarians being taken from their homes by the newly formed secret police, never to be seen again—people like Grandpa, who had been a judge. I lay awake at night fearing the pounding of a rifle on the door.

"I am worried about Grandpa," I confessed to Ivan one day. "Will they come in the night and take him away?"

He knelt in front of me and took me by the shoulders. "Listen, *malka*, don't you worry about that. You go to sleep at night and dream sweet dreams. No one will bother you."

And no one did. But then one day, about a year after the siege began, my soldier had some news. "I am being transferred to another part of the country, *malka*, so I won't be able to come visit anymore," he said. His eyes were clouded with worry. "But I want you to have this," he said, taking something from his pocket. It was a necklace. On it hung a large Russian Orthodox cross with turquoise enamel and a silver border. He placed it around my neck. "God will protect you from harm," he said. I hugged him tight, then watched him drive away.

Not long after, I heard the dreaded knock at the door. The authorities searched for Grandpa, but he had managed to sneak out through a window. After that it was just Grandma and I, trying each day to scrape together enough vegetables from the garden for a meal. Every now and then we received word from Grandpa that he was all right. I wondered where he was hiding and if I would ever see him again. (I had long since given up waiting for Father.) One morning I awoke to find Paprika curled up at my feet, not breathing. *God, why does everyone I love go away?* I asked. The only constant was fear, of starvation, of attack, of losing loved ones. Sometimes I stared at the cross my Russian soldier had given me. Was he back with his own little girl? Did he remember me?

The seasons passed in a haze of anxiety and desperation. Then, in the fall of 1947, a man arrived to tell us he would reunite us with Grandpa at the Austrian border. The ethnic Germans of Hungary were being deported. The man would give us counterfeit papers, passing us off as deportees so we could cross the border to freedom. We traveled all night to get to the meeting place. There, a weary-looking man with a thick, scraggly beard and a knit cap pulled low over his forehead picked me up in his arms. "Grandpa?" I asked, trying to envision the face I used to know. "Yes, it's me, Réni," he answered, planting a bristly kiss on my cheek.

I walked with my grandparents toward the transport trucks, my heart pounding. The coarse burlap sack I carried chafed my hand, and I longed for the softness of Paprika's fur. We got on a flatbed loaded with dozens of people. I wished I could pull my coat over my head and hide from the soldiers who were coming closer to inspect our papers. If we were caught . . . I grabbed Grandpa's hand and squeezed it. *Please, dear God, don't let anything go wrong,* I prayed. *I don't want anything to happen to Grandpa.*

I looked as a guard boarded the truck. I caught my breath. "Grandpa!" I whispered. "It's my soldier! He's checking this truck." I wanted to leap up and run to him, but Grandpa shushed me. "Maybe he won't recognize us," he whispered.

Then my soldier was before us. Grandpa handed over our papers without looking up. I put my hand protectively on his shoulder and peered cautiously at Ivan, hoping to see the old kind sparkle in his eyes. But he was intent upon the papers. I didn't dare breathe. At last he handed the papers back to Grandpa. "Everything is in order in this vehicle," he announced. Then he winked at me. He got down and in an instant our truck was moving on. I looked over my shoulder and caught his eye. "Thank you," I mouthed, holding up the cross hanging around my neck. He nodded discreetly, then turned away. As we passed over the border to safety, I ran my fingers along the intricately cut edges of my cross.

I suffered much sadness during the war, but one blessing will always stay with me: the memory of a kind soldier who made it possible for me and my grandparents to make it to freedom and eventually start new lives in the United States. He turned my fear to faith and showed me that God's compassion can be found anywhere, even in the eyes of an enemy.

If our ears were opened
To hear as angels do
The Intercession-chorus
    arising full and true . . .
We should hear it far up-floating
Beneath the Orient moon,
And catch the golden noting
From the busy Western noon.

~ Frances Ridley Havergal

OLICE FORCE

*"A lot of cops think no one understands them except another cop,"
says William Gillies Kalaidjian, chaplain for the New York Police
Department. And since one hot evening in the summer of 1991, he's
had a new understanding of what that means. That's the night he saw a
legion of "heavenly cops" standing shoulder to shoulder across the
Bronx sky. God's backup forces. Dressed in blue jeans, a few of them
have also come to the aid of an officer in Missouri.*

The Blue Angels

by William Gillies Kalaidjian

ight or wrong, a lot of cops think no one understands them
except another cop. No one but a fellow officer can identify with the incredible pressures of the job: the lonely fear of a midnight foot patrol or the frenzied terror of a high-speed freeway chase;
the stress of deciding in a split second whether a drug-crazed teenager
is pointing a toy gun or a real one; the worry about what will happen to our families should we make the ultimate sacrifice in the line
of duty. Cops like to count on each other first and foremost.

As a chaplain with the New York Police Department for four
decades, I have been both cop and confidant. I've been there with a
cop's family in the emergency room, waiting for the surgeon to tell
us if the officer was going to survive his wounds. I've comforted a patrolman who shot an armed robber and felt terrible about having
harmed another human being. And I've attended too many funerals
for good men and women who died before their time.

I started my career as a foot patrolman, following a stint in the

Navy. Meanwhile I studied for the ministry at Adelphi College and then Union Theological Seminary. After my ordination I was installed as pastor of Bedford Park Congregational Church in the Bronx. But I missed the force and my fellow officers. When the opportunity came to work for the department as a chaplain, I took it.

Being a police chaplain and a full-time pastor hasn't given me a lot of free time through the years, but on a muggy summer night in 1991 I was enjoying a rare evening of relaxation on the porch of our house on 201st Street in the Bronx. As usual I had my portable police radio close at hand, in case I was needed. When I thought I saw a man trying the doors of parked cars lining the still, dark street, I stood up. *Better check it out,* I thought, grabbing my radio. Maybe someone was trying to break into cars. Schools had let out for the year and sometimes kids got into trouble on hot nights.

I proceeded cautiously. Not even the ghost of a breeze disturbed the clammy air. My fingers tightened around the radio as I walked down to the street. If I observed a suspect entering a car, my next move would be to radio a code 10-85 and request quick backup.

Sweat beaded my brow and my clothes clung to me. Stock-still, I stood at the curb. In the dead silence I could hear my heart beating. The thought crossed my mind that I must look awfully vulnerable, standing alone on a dark street. Then, swooshing out of the night, a late-model sedan skidded to a halt directly alongside me. Before I could react, a man leapt out, muscles rippling, and assumed a military crouch. He trained a double-barreled shotgun directly on me and hissed, "Don't move."

I didn't. I barely breathed. The driver, a huge fellow, rushed up and tried to tear off my wristwatch. "Give me your wallet, man," he snarled, shoving me. "Hurry up."

I don't know what got into me. I would normally be the first to say that you should never, ever resist a mugger. Compliance is the safest bet. That's what we always tell civilians. Cash and jewelry are not worth your life. If I had to do it over again, I would just hand over my wallet. But for some reason, that night I got mad. Really mad.

I whacked the thug with my radio. He cursed me, enraged. I swung at him again, and he charged me like a mad bull, hurling me into a fence nearby. I hit with a thud. Air exploded out of my lungs. I heard him scream at his partner, "Shoot him! Kill him!" I waited for the two big muzzles to blaze and shotgun pellets to rip through me.

Bullets travel faster than sound, and as any cop who has survived a shooting will tell you, you feel the bullet before you hear the shot. But I felt and heard nothing. I looked skyward and immediately saw the most awesome sight of my life—a phalanx of policemen. They hovered above, standing out against the dark Bronx sky. A legion of blue-uniformed men, shoulder to shoulder in close deep ranks, shoes spit-polished, sterling shields and silver wings gleaming. Angels on patrol, heavenly cops to the rescue.

I thought quickly, *Yea, though I walk through the valley of the shadow of death, I will fear no evil* (Psalm 23:4, KJV), and all fear left me. I felt as though I were standing with God. My attackers seemed to be frozen in place. Words came to me silently but forcefully: *Call for backup. Now!*

Radio in hand, I looked the perpetrator directly in the eye and pressed the call button. "This is the police chaplain," I shouted. "Ten-thirteen at Two hundred first and Bainbridge, ten-thirteen, ten-thirteen!" The 10-13 code would alert every cop in the borough that a fellow officer was in trouble. Almost instantly the night erupted with screaming sirens. To my ears it was a symphony. As the angels above faded, patrol cars converged on Bainbridge Avenue, lights flashing. My attackers dove into their car and tore off down the street, tires squealing. I jumped in the back of the first squad car that swooped up, and we took off in hot pursuit. We lost them but put out an all-points-bulletin on their tags. In less than half an hour the men were taken into custody. Eventually they were sentenced to hard time upstate.

Nothing is more reassuring to a police officer than knowing he can get backup when he's in trouble, that other cops will be there when he calls. I know. I found out for myself one hot night in the Bronx, when God sent in His backup.

"Lord, You Can Kick in Anytime"

by Doris Smith

*U*niform on, I was about to leave the house when my four-year-old grandson Nathaniel, who was visiting us for the weekend, stopped me. In a plaintive voice he asked, "Are you coming home, Grandma?"

"Of course, honey," I said, strapping on my waist holster. I was surprised at his concern. My job as a deputy for the Miller County Sheriff's Department can be dangerous, but on that September day I wasn't particularly worried about my assignment. I had to take a prisoner from the jail two counties over to another facility in the northeastern part of Missouri. I actually looked forward to transporting prisoners; it meant a respite from the day-to-day routine of my job. But Nathaniel's eyes still looked serious, so I gave him a hug before I went out to my patrol car.

On the way to the Callaway County jail, I reviewed the information the dispatcher had given me. The prisoner in question was serving a sentence for writing bad checks. Because of minor medical and behavior problems, she was being transferred to Palmyra, about a hundred seventy-five miles away.

At Callaway County I picked her up, a slight woman around twenty-five. She hardly looked like a dangerous criminal. Still, I had to follow regulations and secure her in the backseat of my Chevrolet Caprice. Even as I fastened a belt of nylon webbing around her waist, handcuffed her to the belt and put her in leg shackles, she was pleasant and cooperative. *She won't be any problem*, I thought.

I pulled onto Highway 54, heading north, glad it was a gorgeous late-summer afternoon. An hour later, I was in Audrain County, right on schedule, when out of the corner of my eye I noticed the prisoner had leaned forward in her seat. Thinking she was going to speak to me, I cocked my head in her direction.

Her hands thrust through the small, thirteen-inch-wide window in the Plexiglas partition separating me from the backseat. She was out of the cuffs!

"Get back!" I shouted, adrenaline rushing through me.

She kept coming. Amazingly, she squeezed her head and upper body through the partition window. Spitting out a stream of curses, she flailed her arms. I tried to keep my eyes on the road and evade her blows at the same time, but the seat belt confined me. Finally I hit the brakes and stopped my car in the middle of the road. Fortunately there was no traffic in sight.

"Get back!" I yelled again, pushing at her with my hands as I twisted around, the seat belt pressing on my chest.

She reached for my hand-held radio on the armrest to my right. Grabbing its antenna, she swung it toward my head, knocking my glasses off. I ducked, and the radio fell to the floorboard.

Disoriented, I tried to regain my bearings. She lunged forward again and bit my left hand. I screamed in pain. It felt as if my hand had been smashed with a red-hot hammer. I struggled to defend myself. The prisoner was totally out of control, like a wild animal.

All at once I sensed a change. The prisoner seemed to pause. Immediately, instinctively, I knew why. *She's going for my gun!* I braced my right hand on my holster as she made a desperate grab. We wrestled over the holster. I tried to knock her away with my elbow, but she didn't stop. I heard the snap give, and the next thing I knew, she had yanked out my nine-millimeter Glock.

I don't want to die in my car, I thought. The faces of my husband and our children and grandchildren flashed in my mind. *I want to go home to my family.*

I have always believed in God. I knew I had to call on Him now. "Lord, You can kick in anytime," I said under my breath as I frantically fought for control of the Glock. I kept both hands on the gun, desperate to keep the trigger covered. If the prisoner managed to deactivate the safety mechanism in the center of the trigger, it would all be over. *Lord . . .*

Something told me to look to the front of my patrol car. Through the windshield I saw two figures running toward me. Without my glasses, I couldn't make out much more than their blurry shapes. But

I knew they were men of average height and build, dressed in white T-shirts and blue jeans.

One of them tried to get in the car, but the doors were locked. The other banged on the hood. The prisoner looked up, distracted, and loosened her grip on the gun. I freed my left hand and flipped the autolock button forward. Quickly the man standing by the rear driver's-side door opened it and pulled the prisoner back through the partition window. Catching my breath, I reholstered my weapon and stepped out of my car. With the men's help, I once again secured the prisoner in the backseat. She was kicking and spitting so violently, I took extra precautions and shackled her arms to her feet.

"Thanks, guys," I told my helpers as I got back behind the wheel. My hands were still trembling as I pulled off the road into a nearby driveway. I took out my radio and called for backup.

After making sure the prisoner was staying put, I got out to speak with my rescuers. To my shock, they were gone. There was no trace of them. In fact, there was no one—no cars, no people—on the straightaway stretch of highway still in view.

While I tried to figure out how they could have vanished, officers from the Audrain County Sheriff's Department and the Missouri State Highway Patrol arrived. I asked if they had seen the two men. They shook their heads. The only sighting was reported by the woman whose driveway I had pulled into. Hearing the commotion outside, she ran to the window and spotted two men in jeans. "Don't worry, I got pictures of them," she promised. Eager to capture the excitement of the scene, she had grabbed her camera and snapped several pictures of the men from the safety of her house. Then she watched them drive away in a blue truck. When her film was developed, however, they did not appear in any of the photographs. Neither did the blue truck.

Over the next few days, my boss, Sheriff Strobe, made countless inquiries to identify the two men in jeans, all to no avail. The local newspaper printed an article asking them to come forward to be recognized for their valor. Similar requests went out over the airwaves from radio stations in the area. There was never any response.

To this day, I have no idea who they were. All I know is this: God kicked in just in time to save my life. That's enough for me.

 UIET

"Sometimes God sends angels to help us accept life's tragedies and find a way to make good come of them." That's what Carol Lee Hughes learned, having found that comfort in the quiet music of a windup toy. And young Jeremy in the second grade, overwhelmed with grief for his mother—well, his quiet angelic message will encourage you in the midst of any sad season.

Autumn's Christmas Bear

by Carol Lee Hughes

utumn Grace came to us when Ted and I were facing the empty-nest years, with four older children married or away at college. We didn't know what to expect, starting over with a baby again. But how quickly we fell into the routines of early parenthood, juggling schedules of who had to be where when. Ted's hours as an engineer were reasonably steady, and I cut back on my courses at a regional campus of the University of Wisconsin, where I was a professor of language arts. Our home was in Oak Creek, and I found a wonderful baby-sitter who lived between our home and my workplace.

In the blink of an eye our sleepy newborn grew into an inquisitive toddler. She followed me around the house like a curious duckling, getting into everything. Only one thing could keep her still. Books. Autumn had her favorites—*Carl's Christmas* and *Goodnight,*

Moon—and I had mine. We read them all. *The Polar Express* was way beyond her comprehension, but she listened to every word. It must have been my enthusiastic delivery. I was amazed when she began to pick out letters, especially capital A. "For 'Autumn,' " we said together.

One chilly winter evening we curled up on the couch to read. "Mooooon," Autumn cooed at the big, round face in the blue sky, picking the book she wanted to read first. Next came the one about a rottweiler named Carl. Carl reminded her of our mixed-breed Labrador, Orion. Autumn planted her chubby little index finger on Carl's hefty figure, calling him Orion before I turned each page.

If Autumn was going to be a lifelong reader, to have the world opened up to her through the written word, I had to let her fall in love with books on her own. I lined up books on low shelves around the house, stuck them under the bedroom dresser, even put some in a bottom kitchen cabinet, places where Autumn could discover them herself. There were always books within her reach, and she often plunked herself down on the floor to "read" one. Poring over the pages, she played the part of serious student. And then one day I heard her, in a mixture of babbling and recognizable two- and three-word phrases, mimicking the pauses and intonations of expressive reading. She was developing her own reading voice!

As winter deepened Ted, Autumn and I spent more time in front of the fireplace, Autumn in her wooden rocker, holding her stuffed Christmas bear. Ever since her grandmother had given it to her, on her very first Christmas, Autumn hadn't spent a night without that bear. She loved it. When she pressed its paw a hidden computer chip played music. Sometimes Autumn pressed the paw once too often, and I hoped I'd never hear the carols it played again. Autumn's second Christmas had passed, but I knew there was no chance of her letting me put the bear away until next year.

Only days after her second birthday, Autumn and I were driving to her baby-sitter's when we were in a car accident. I don't remember the crash itself, but I was aware enough to know that ambulance attendants were loading me into a Flight for Life. They were not loading my daughter.

Ted got to the hospital while I was being prepped for surgery.

"Autumn . . ." I whispered. Ted held me tight. "The ambulance has arrived," he said. "We can hold her."

We cradled our little girl, hugging her gently, telling her good-bye, though we knew she was already gone.

From a hospital bed, winter seemed even harsher. My operation, the pain, the physical therapy, even the signs of healing—all pointed up the awful fact that I was alive while my daughter, who had been in my care, was not. I spent hours staring out the window at a cruel and capricious world. *Why, God?* I finally asked one day, the question breaking a dam of grief and anger. *Why did You give us Autumn only to snatch her away? Where was her guardian angel while mine saved me? Or aren't angels real at all?*

Just then Ted walked in. I wasn't much for making conversation those days, and there weren't words for my sadness anyway. Ted seemed to accept my silence. He came and sat beside me on the bed.

"I'm not going to get well," I told him. "Even if I could, I wouldn't."

My husband studied my eyes as if he were trying to see our future in them. He looked so tired. "Carol Lee, if you don't make it through this, I won't either."

Ted was careful with his words; he didn't say things unless he truly meant them. For the first time since the accident I felt something besides my own pain: I was sad for him too. "I'm so sorry, Ted. You lost Autumn too. We'll get through this together."

I went to God to ask for strength. It was a relief to pray without anger and bitterness, to open myself to His graces. I also tried to put words to my sadness. Writing had always been a kind of therapy for me. Maybe it could help me now. I wrote a poem with the line, "No life so small that it cannot change the world." After that the questions I brought to God took a different turn: *How did Autumn's life make a difference? How can it continue to make a difference?*

Shuffling around my bedroom after I got home from the hospital, I accidentally knocked over a pile of Autumn's books. I wanted to leave evidence of Autumn scattered around the house—her books, her wooden rocker, her Christmas bear. I would never let her disappear from our lives. Holding her favorite *Goodnight, Moon,* I wondered, *How can Autumn touch other lives too?*

I went to the phone and dialed information. "Children's Hospital of Wisconsin," I requested. There was only one children's hospital in the entire state, and it happened to be in Milwaukee, adjacent to the hospital where Autumn and I had been taken.

"Do you have any permanent provision for buying books?" I asked the children's support director, who took my call.

"I'm afraid not," she said. "Cutbacks have hit us hard, and buying medical equipment comes first. It's a shame, though."

That night I talked to Ted. "If Autumn had been able to recover in the hospital," I told him, "we both know what she would have spent most of her time doing." And that was the start of the Autumn Grace Hughes Fund, to provide hospitalized youngsters with books. We let family and friends know how they could help keep Autumn's spirit alive. Donations came in, some as small as fifty cents. Months passed, and the fund grew as word of our mission spread. I put in our first order at the local bookstore. We had bookplates made with a photo of Autumn reading, taken just weeks before her death.

Already it had been nearly a year since that awful day. I still had dark moments when my faith wavered and I asked the hard questions all over again. Was there a loving God? Had I started this fund to help other children, or was it a desperate way to hang on to my own child? In the end I always chose to believe that there were messengers between heaven and earth, that Autumn was alive with God, and that she'd be very pleased to share her love of books with other children. I *had* to believe.

Deep inside, though, I wished I *knew.*

December 20 was the day I'd arranged to drop off the very first donations from the fund. The snowy night before, Orion and I were the only ones home. I let the dog in, and started a fire while he shook himself off by the door. "There, now," I said, gazing into the flames, "this'll warm us up."

Autumn had always been mesmerized by our fires. This was the first one built since she'd died. Ted had put her little wooden rocker a safe distance from the crackling embers, and now her Christmas bear sat there looking on. I straightened the bear's hat and smoothed its sweatshirt. The chair continued to rock for a moment after my fussing. I would have given anything for Autumn to squeeze that bear paw and start the music. I couldn't even remember which carols it played. I had to smile, remembering how attached Autumn had been to that bear, and later I went up to bed with happy thoughts of her.

I awoke the next morning feeling different. Gone was the sadness that had dulled most of my days since Autumn died. I passed over the drab clothes I'd been wearing all year; I reached in the back of my closet for a skirt with bright snowflakes on it. "Today," I told myself, "is my Christmas day." I dressed and went downstairs.

There on the table, in neat stacks, were brand-new hardcover copies of *The Polar Express, The Littlest Angel, Carl's Christmas* and *Goodnight, Moon.* All ready for the children at the hospital. I checked the envelope holding the bookplates and hoped we had enough. Then I heard Orion scratching to be let in.

"Cold out there, boy?" I asked, opening the back door. Orion stepped inside and, fastidious as usual, stood on the mat shaking himself off and cleaning the snow from his paws. I remembered I'd left the chimney flue open and crossed the room to the hearth. As I leaned into the fireplace to pull the flue, I heard it. Distinctly. Music. A Christmas carol, "The First Noel."

I turned, stunned.

On the little wooden rocker Autumn's Christmas bear sat perfectly still, the chair motionless. The bear was playing a carol.

But who had pressed its paw?

"The angel did say . . ." came the bear's song.

I looked over at Orion, who hadn't moved from the back door. No one else was in the house. The carol played through, and the music stopped.

Finally I *knew.* I didn't have the answers to all my hard questions, but I knew for sure that angels are real. Sometimes God sends them to help us accept life's tragedies and find a way to make good come of them. Autumn was alive with God in heaven, and her short life on earth would continue to make a difference. With new purpose, I picked up the books and headed for the door. The children were waiting.

Never Alone

by Jane Mitchell*

On our refrigerator is a crayon drawing of an angel with curly hair and blue eyes, and whenever things seem too much to handle, I look at it and remember how much my family, especially my grandson Jeremy, has overcome. He was only two years old when my daughter, Mary, took him and his four-year-old sister, Sarah, and left her abusive, alcoholic husband.

Shortly after settling into her own apartment, Mary began feeling so fatigued she couldn't keep up with basic household tasks. Soon she and the kids had to move in with her father, Frank, and me, while the doctors tried to figure out what was wrong. I thought perhaps she was overwhelmed by all she had been through and just needed rest. But the doctors made a devastating discovery. Mary suffered from a fatal degenerative muscle disease.

Mary fought hard to keep caring for the kids, just as I threw all my energy into caring for her. She dragged herself to school functions even when she was too tired to dress herself. She gave the children baths till she couldn't muster the strength to turn on the faucet. The children instinctively understood and were always ready to clean up around the house or bring her a glass of water. Sarah slept with her every night, and Mary's lap seemed the only place where bubbly Jeremy would sit still. It was a struggle to coax the kids to leave her and go to school. Mary would watch them through the window till they were out of sight.

But one morning when I came into her room after the kids had gone and Frank had left for work, Mary wasn't in her usual spot. I found her huddled under her blankets, sobbing so hard she could hardly catch her breath.

"What is it, honey?" I asked. Thinking she was in pain, I scanned the bottles of pills arrayed on her night table, wondering which medicine might help her.

*Name has been changed.

Gasping, she said, "The children told me this morning." I waited for her to collect herself. "All this time I thought their father only took his temper out on me. But, oh, Mom, I was wrong. He hurt them too. Why didn't I leave sooner?"

I sat on the bed and pulled her onto my lap. "You're here now, sweetie," I said. "You're with us." How well I understood the helplessness she felt, unable to protect her own children. I wished I could wrap her in my arms and shield her always, from the past that had caused her so much pain and from the future that would bring her more.

Eventually Mary was on oxygen round-the-clock, her entire body swollen due to medication. When she fell asleep I sat facing the window, where the glow of the streetlight filtered through the sheer curtains in the shape of a cross, and prayed for strength. One afternoon Mary looked in my eyes and said, "Mom, I'm not going to be here much longer. What are we going to do about the children?"

I took her hand. "I promise you, Sarah and Jeremy will never be hurt again," I said.

Barely a month later, on an August morning, I drove Mary to the doctor for a regular appointment. Her doctor said she should go straight to the hospital, but she insisted on going home first to see the kids. When the ambulance arrived for Mary, the children, now eight and six, wrapped her weak arms around themselves, not wanting to let go. At the hospital the doctors gave her fluids, oxygen and painkillers, but she kept getting worse. Before I knew it, the flurry of white coats ended, and I held my daughter as she took her last breath.

In the car on the way home I felt as if a fog had rolled into my mind, shrouding every thought but one: How would I tell the kids?

Sarah and Jeremy were sprawled on their mother's empty bed, drawing pictures. I sat down between them.

"Jeremy, Sarah . . . Grandma has something to tell you." I took a deep breath and gathered them close to me. "Mommy won't be coming home. She's gone to heaven."

Sarah recoiled from my touch, screaming, "No, Mommy's not gone!" It took some time for Frank and me to calm her. When I turned to find Jeremy, I saw him curled up in a corner, the bright crayon colors of his drawing dulled by tears.

The next couple of weeks Frank and I went through the motions—accepting condolences, making arrangements, talking little except to soothe the kids. The initial outpouring of sympathy from friends and neighbors gradually tapered off, and we were left alone with our grief. I awoke the morning the kids were to return to school just wanting to pull the covers over my head and stay in bed forever. "Come on, Jane," Frank shook me gently, "first day of school. We have to get the kids up." *Yes, he's right, the kids need me. I have to keep going.* When Sarah and Jeremy left, I watched them from the window as Mary used to do.

That afternoon I asked Jeremy, "So how is first grade? What did you do today?" He showed me a gray page from his writing tablet with the words, "I love my mom. She was the best mom in the world. I miss my mom."

When I went to tuck him in that night, he lay facing the wall, weeping. I turned him over and stroked his hair. He rubbed his eyes with his fists and said, "I miss Mommy's lap." I lay down and put my arm around him, unable to hold back my own tears. "I know, Jeremy," I said. "I miss her too."

Both kids got counseling to help them deal with the abuse they'd suffered and their mother's death. It seemed Sarah was slowly getting back to normal, but not Jeremy. *Give it time,* I told myself. But weeks turned into months and Jeremy continued to cling to me during the day and cry quietly at night. I was overwhelmed by the same helplessness I had felt watching Mary waste away. Jeremy was in more pain than ever, and there was nothing I could do. I went to bed each night with his sobs echoing in my ears, feeling like a failure for not being able to keep my promise to my daughter.

One day Jeremy's teacher called. "His grades keep getting worse," she said, "and he has crying spells in class when nothing I say can comfort him. I wish I could figure out what to do for him." *Me too,* I thought. I looked at Jeremy's drawings displayed on the refrigerator door: Mary's grave, hearts with the word *Mom* in them, he and his mother hand in hand. *God, please, we can't go on like this.*

That night, when I went into his room to dry his tears, I said, "Jeremy, I know how sad you are about Mommy. But maybe it will help to remember the good times we had with her. What do you remember?"

His face lit up. "She bought me . . ." He named a popular set of toys. *How long has it been since I've done anything special for him?*

I began taking him on more outings. He'd seem happy for a while, but then something would set him off, like an old photograph of Mary or friends talking about their moms, and the crying fits would start up again. He barely passed first grade. I could feel him being swept away by a sorrow that was too big for him—and me—to fight.

One summer night I sat in the family room, looking through a parenting magazine for ideas on how to reach Jeremy. I closed it as he padded up to me in his pajamas, his face puffy and red. "Grandma," he announced, "I want to go be with Mommy right now."

I gave him a hug. "Sweetheart, I want to see her too," I said. "But she's in heaven."

"Then I want to die so I can be with her."

I held him away from me and squeezed his bony shoulders. "Honey, listen to me. You can't. It's not your time to go to heaven yet."

"But I miss Mommy."

I took him back to bed. "Jeremy," I said, smoothing the blanket around him, "I know I'm not your mommy, but I love you and I promise to help you."

I returned to the family room and sat in my old spot, facing the cross of light on the curtains. *Father, You've promised You wouldn't give us more than we could handle. Well, this little boy has been abused, and he's lost his mother. He's so young, Father, and he can't handle it. Not by himself.*

I heard Jeremy's voice faintly calling and raced to his room. "Grandma, come here," he said, motioning for me to sit next to him on the bed. I noticed his eyes were shining, though not with tears.

"Grandma," he whispered, "I just saw my guardian angel."

"What?"

"He was floating right over my bed."

"What did he look like?" I asked.

"He had on a shiny white robe, and his hair was curly. His eyes were really blue. And he had wings." I had never heard Jeremy so serious, so confident.

"Did he say anything?"

"He said God was watching over me."

"Yes, he is, Jeremy," I said softly. "And so am I."

Jeremy was very peaceful during the following weeks, but when it came time for him to start second grade I was worried about whether the change would hold. Then one afternoon his teacher called. "Mrs. Mitchell," she said, "I wanted to let you know that the students handed in papers for an essay contest." *Oh, no,* I thought, picturing another writing tablet full of "I miss my mom."

"Jeremy wrote about an experience he had this summer—when he saw an angel," she said. "His paper was selected as the winner from the entire second grade!"

I knew then that things had truly turned around for my grandson. Four years later, the angel Jeremy drew for the cover of his essay remains on the refrigerator. I have come to think of Jeremy's angel as my angel too. He is a reminder that God keeps his promises—and will help me keep mine.

OADWAY

Most days most of us leave our homes and walk, ride or drive along roads, one leading to another, the network taking us from "here" to "there" and back again. Usually we know exactly where we're going. But sometimes we get twisted around, tooling down a road that's taking us . . . we don't know where.

The same thing happens on the roadway of life: Sometimes we get lost. And then God just might send along a stranger who gives good directions for getting back on course . . . if we're paying attention.

Daddy and the Drifter

by Valerie Capps-Walton

My daddy was a hardworking, outgoing man who loved to sing and tell stories; he was well liked by everybody in our small Missouri town. But he was also a big drinker and had an eye for the ladies.

Some of my earliest memories are of our Saturday outings. They were always the same. Every few weeks he drove me into town in Betsy, our Model A Ford, to see the new western playing at the movie house. Then we went to the general store for groceries to supplement the food we grew on our farm. After that we stopped at one or both of the local taverns, and he sat at the bar drinking while I played in a corner or talked to some of the customers. The sky was usually chock-full of stars by the time we left. Daddy swerved the car drunk-enly from side to side on the bumpy gravel road, and I braced myself against the dashboard, wishing we could just get home.

But there was still one more stop—a run-down frame house on the outskirts of town. "Be ri' back, sweetie pie—you juss sit tight," he'd murmur, but he was always gone a long time, and I was left alone to stare at the dark fields of wheat swaying in the breeze. Occasionally I'd hear a woman's high-pitched giggle above the chirp of crickets. When I saw him coming back, I'd curl up in a corner of the big back-seat and pretend I was asleep.

At home, Daddy would stumble through the door reeking of whiskey and cheap perfume, and I'd hurry to crawl into bed with my younger brothers and sisters. Mama would cry and plead, Daddy would curse and yell, and I'd pull the blanket over my head and try to think about the movie we'd seen.

The following morning Mama would get us all up and off to church early. Daddy would stand in the doorway and call after us. "Don't you all go down there a-prayin' for me. Now, I mean it," he would shout. "I don't want those do-gooders a-beggin' for my soul, ya hear me?"

At church Mama ignored his warnings. "Lord, he's a good man," she'd pray. "Steer him away from liquor and show him the right path." Sometimes the whole congregation echoed her plea for my daddy. Week after week, month after month, they asked God to send my daddy guidance. But his Saturday escapades continued, until one hot, muggy afternoon in the summer of 1955.

We had just turned onto the main road into town. I tried not to think about how the day would inevitably end, keeping my mind on the gentle weight of Daddy's arm around my shoulder at the matinee, the smell of buttered popcorn and which candy I'd pick out at the store afterward. The damp heat had plastered my shirt against my body. I rolled down the window and stuck my face out in the breeze. That's when I saw him. A man dressed in baggy pants and a white shirt with sleeves rolled up halfway to his elbows was walking slowly along the side of the road. His dark hair was a little shaggy, and he needed a shave. "Daddy, look," I called. We didn't get many strangers in town.

"Get yourself inside, sweetie pie," Daddy said, tugging at my shoulder. "I see him." He pulled to the side of the road and waited. The man ambled up to the open window and, without a glance at me, gazed directly at my father.

"Howdy," Daddy said to the man, who kept staring at him with the most penetrating blue eyes. Daddy squirmed a bit in his seat and gave a strained smile. "Hop in and we'll give you a lift into town. 'Tain't a fit day for man nor beast to be walkin' in this heat."

The man opened the door and slid into the seat beside me. I scooted close to Daddy and warily eyed our passenger. He still hadn't said a word.

Daddy shifted Betsy into gear and eased back onto the deserted road. I'd never known him to be so quiet with company.

At last the stranger began to speak, his voice soft and melodic. He and Daddy made small talk about the weather, the scenery, the car—nothing special. Soon I relaxed. I tuned out and wondered how to convince Daddy to stop at the drugstore for strawberry malteds before the movie. Then there was a change in Daddy's tone that snapped me to attention.

"What do you mean by that?" Daddy asked suspiciously.

"Sometimes in the course of everyday living we lose sight of what is right and what is wrong," the stranger responded quietly. "We don't mean to do it, but so often we push God aside. But everyone deserves a second chance, don't you agree?"

Oh, no, I thought, *there goes my malted.* Nothing ruined Daddy's mood quicker than preaching.

I cringed, waiting for the explosion. When it didn't come, I squinted up at Daddy. He had the oddest look.

"Let me off up there." The drifter motioned toward a dirt path that intersected the road. Daddy stopped the car and the man stepped out.

He smiled kindly at Daddy. "The good Lord willing, I'll be seeing you again in a couple of years, Clarence." He stuffed his hands in his pockets and walked a short distance away, then paused and glanced back over his shoulder. He looked at me, and I felt a warmth that had nothing to do with the weather. Then he again gazed at Daddy.

"Wait ten minutes before you drive on," he said. We watched him disappear into the nearby woods.

"Who was he?" I asked Daddy, realizing there had been no intro-ductions. "How'd he know your name?"

"I don't know," Daddy frowned as he checked his pocket watch and shifted into gear. "Just some fool, I reckon." It was clear Daddy didn't want to discuss it further.

Betsy lurched twice, sputtered, and died. Daddy hit the starter. The car caught for a second, then died again. Cursing, Daddy got under the hood and jiggled some wires, then came back and tried again. Nothing happened. Daddy sat back and stared through the windshield. I waited for him to speak, smile, swear, do something—but there was no sound except our breathing.

Finally Daddy sighed and tried again to start the car. This time the engine purred immediately. Daddy checked his watch and muttered as we started moving. We rode in silence for a while. As we crested the hill near the Miller farm, a black cloud of smoke shot up from the road directly ahead. Daddy slammed the brakes, and we skidded to a stop. Mr. Miller walked over to Daddy's side. "Truck came 'round the corner too fast. Terrible thing," Mr. Miller said, his voice trem-bling as he watched the flames sear the already torrid air. He pulled a grimy handkerchief from a pocket and wiped his forehead. "Just happened 'bout ten minutes ago."

Daddy clutched the steering wheel so tightly his knuckles turned white. He stared ahead, seemingly transfixed by the inferno. After a few moments he looked at me, his face ashen. He drew me close against his chest, hiding my face from the blaze.

We never made it to town that day. Daddy turned around and headed home. He didn't say a word the whole way, and I was the one who told Mama about the wreck. Something held me back from mentioning the stranger. Daddy and I never talked about him either. But Daddy was never the same after that hot summer day. We kept up our Saturday movie ritual, but I never saw him get drunk or visit that old frame house again. He even started going to church with us. Occasionally he still let loose a string of cuss words, but afterward he'd look skyward and mutter sheepishly, "Sorry, Lord. It's like I told You, I'm a-tryin', but I ain't no saint."

Soon after his meeting with the drifter, Daddy was baptized in a creek. Folks from miles around came out for it. I can't remember ever

seeing Mama happier than during the next two years before Daddy died.

"I'll be seeing you again in a couple years," the drifter had said. I thought back to that day as I sat beside Mama at the funeral home. And I finally told her about it. When I was finished, she smiled and hugged me. "Your daddy was a very lucky man, honey," she said. "He got to talk to an angel right here on this earth!"

O passing angel . . .

rouse me to the race and make me strong.

~ Christina Rossetti

"They Call Me Quarter Horse"

by Wayne Herndon

Wayne, how fast are you going?" my wife, Susan, asked for what seemed like the hundredth time on the run to Bakersfield, California. "You'll get a ticket!" I gripped the wheel, trying not to lose my temper. What was I thinking when I agreed to team up with her on this trip? She had her trucker's license too—that's how we met. But I'd been driving a rig for eighteen years. I knew what I was doing.

I kept my eyes on the road and my foot on the pedal. The tension between Susan and me had been building since we left Oregon more than eighteen hours ago, and I'd long since clammed up rather than talk about what the problem was. "I'm going to the back to read," Susan finally announced. The curtains that separated the sleeper berth from the front seats closed with an impatient snap. We would be in Bakersfield in about two hours, but I wasn't sure if we'd last that long together.

I continued down Interstate 5, pulling a refrigerator trailer with Kennesaw emblazoned on the sides. There were no other trucks around, so I gave a holler on the CB. "Breaker one-nine," I broadcast onto channel nineteen, the station most truckers use.

"Go ahead, break," a voice immediately answered. "What's your handle?"

"Bodyguard," I told him, happy to have some friendly company.

"They call me Quarter Horse," the trucker said. We exchanged information about our locations. Quarter Horse was about a mile ahead. "How you doing?" he asked.

A truck whizzed by me on the left, and I thought of Susan's nagging about my driving. "Not so good," I admitted. Something in the man's voice had put me at ease, and I wanted to talk. "I'm part of a driving team this run, and it's been . . . well, it's been hard."

Being a trucker, Quarter Horse knew all about the regulations forbidding drivers to run more than ten hours in twenty-four. By teaming up with a partner, you could move your truck twice as far each day, switching on and off at the wheel. It was more efficient, but it meant being cooped up with another person for hours, even days on end. There is no privacy, no space and, of course, no shower in a truck. "You been getting on each other's nerves?" Quarter Horse asked.

I told him I was driving team with my wife. Before I could catch myself, I was going on about how much I loved Susan but couldn't seem to show it. I didn't want to argue with her over speed limits or keeping the truck clean, but I didn't know how to stop. "Quarter Horse, I just don't know what I'm doing wrong."

"I used to feel the same way," he admitted. "So when my wife told me it was either counseling or divorce, you better believe I went to counseling. I learned I had to treat my wife—and myself—with respect."

I thought about the way I treated Susan. I hadn't ever raised my voice to her. What else could I do? "How do I treat my wife with more respect?"

"You've got to trust her," Quarter Horse said simply. "Trust her judgment enough to listen to what she's saying. Trust that she loves you."

On the road a man learns to look out for himself. Trusting someone else—even someone I loved—didn't come all that easy.

My truck was approaching the last rest stop before Bakersfield when Quarter Horse said he was signing off and named his mile marker. *Still just a mile ahead,* I thought. Although I had been trying for the past hour, for some reason I hadn't been able to catch up to him.

"Thanks, Quarter Horse. I'll give it some thought."

A new voice broke in on the CB. "Hey, Kennesaw," he said. "I hear you talking, but I don't know who to. I passed you earlier, and it's been clear up the road since. Ain't nobody else on it."

That was when I realized the voice I had heard over the CB was no ordinary truck driver. I pulled into the rest stop, popped the brakes and stepped into the sleeping berth. Susan looked up from her book, tensed for another fight. Then her expression softened. "What is it, Wayne?" she asked.

Gently, I took the book from her hands, saving her place with a scrap of paper. "Honey," I said, taking her hands in mine, "we need to talk."

Susan looked at me without a trace of anger. She was ready to listen. Was I really ready to talk honestly? "Trust her," Quarter Horse had said. I took a deep breath.

"Honey, I'm sorry for being so stubborn," I said. "I have a hard time trusting people, but I don't mean you any disrespect. From now on things are going to be different."

"Oh, Wayne, I'm sorry too!" she said, her eyes filling with tears. She threw her arms around me and held me for a long time. The rest of the trip seemed like a vacation.

I'm driving alone again now, while Susan stays at home with our baby. Sometimes I'll run into couples driving team, getting on each other's nerves. I tell them about respect and trust. I'm not an angel myself, but I can try to share the message given to me by one called Quarter Horse.

TORE

Whether we're stocking shelves or running a cash register, browsing for just the right gift or buying a week's groceries, we are not left on our own in the marketplace. Our angels are near—to guard and guide.

Convenience Store Robbery

by Karen Davis

After dark one night in March, I walked into the convenience store in Paducah, Kentucky, where I was a cashier. I stopped just inside the door while my eyes adjusted to the bright fluorescent lights. It was my second week on the job. I still had jitters about the late-night stints, but I knew I was lucky to have found work at all.

The year so far had been rough. My son had been in a serious car accident, and my husband had to have leg surgery, twice. I watched the medical bills pile up after my employer downsized me out of a job. Finding a new one hadn't been easy. It seemed that every business in our town was laying off instead of hiring. Just as I was losing hope, I applied at a gas station/convenience store not far from my house. When the manager saw I had experience operating a cash register, he said, "We need someone for afternoons and relief midnights. Interested?"

How could I say no?

The daytime hours, with a constant flow of customers, suited me just fine, but I had counted the minutes on that first night shift. Besides being fearful of the late, dark hours, I disliked the long stretches all by myself. Customers were in and out in a jiffy, rushing home to watch TV or go to bed. Now here I was again, ready to start the lonely countdown, trying to remain cheerful as I said good-bye to the cashier who preceded me. Checking my register drawer and the bags of extra coins, I settled in for the night. I was on my own.

Still, I *had* found a job, I reminded myself, straightening the colorful cigarette lighters behind the counter. I had faith the Lord was looking out for me. Wasn't He? Sometimes I wondered if even He had lost sight of me, tucked away in this bright, white beacon off the road.

Around 10:45 P.M. a customer came in to pay for gas, then went out and filled his tank. When he was done, he came back inside. "Waiting in the car, my daughter saw a man in the alley alongside the store," he said. "It's probably nothing, but we thought we should tell you."

I followed him to the door and looked around. Nothing seemed amiss. "Thank you anyway," I said to the customer before he drove away.

Preferring to err on the side of caution, I hid the bags of rolled coins under the register and locked the side of the safe for which I had the combination. I watched out the big plate-glass window for a while, my eyes following the occasional pair of headlights passing in the darkness. *If anything happened to me in here, who would know?*

To take my mind off my fear, I concentrated on restocking the shelves. Neatly stacking soup cans, I reminded the Lord that I needed His protection. By the time I got to the cookies, I had forgotten all about the goings-on outside.

Until I looked up from the shelf to see a gun pointed at my face.

Holding it was a tall, thin man wearing dirty tennis shoes, jeans, a sweat jacket and a ski cap. A blue bandanna hid his nose and mouth.

Reflexively I put my hands in the air. "Jesus, help me!" I cried.

"The money," the man growled, waving his weapon toward the register. I held my hands high, hoping someone outside would notice.

I'm kidding myself. It's late. There was no one outside, no one to help.

"Get your hands down!" the man said, and followed me through the aisle.

I moved slowly, not wanting to provoke him. He pushed me behind the counter and crouched down so he couldn't be seen from the street. "Open the register!" he demanded. His eyes flickered with menace.

Trembling violently, I did as he said. *How bad would a bullet hurt?* I wondered. My fingers fumbled with the keys. *Am I going to die?*

The drawer sprang open. Keeping low, the man reached up and grabbed the cash. Then he got to his feet. We were face-to-face, only inches separating us. In that instant everything changed.

It was no longer just the two of us in the store. We had company. *Thank You, Lord.*

Hovering above my assailant was a huge unearthly presence. I knew I was finally seeing something that had been there all along, watching out for me. Suddenly, although my assailant didn't know it, the balance of power shifted.

"Now open the safe," he ordered.

"I don't have the combination," I said evenly. This was half true. I only had the combination to part of it.

"Don't mess with me, lady!"

"I don't have the combination," I repeated calmly. The robber saw the change in me. Unnerved, he jostled the money bag, which contained less than two hundred dollars. He wanted more.

"Where's your purse?" he said finally, desperate to finish this job.

My purse was in the office. I glanced at the office door, which stood ajar. *What should I do?* I didn't want the man to follow me in there. I stared at the robber defiantly.

The phone rang, interrupting our standoff. "If I don't answer, the caller will know something's wrong," I said quickly. With that, the man ran from the store.

I grabbed the phone. "I've been robbed!" I said.

A 911 operator was on the line. "It has been reported," she assured me. "Police units are on the way."

Then I heard shouting in the back alley and the squeal of tires. Sirens blared. As a squad car pulled up in front of the store, I looked around inside. My angel was gone.

As it turned out, I had been far from alone that night. Sonny Fondaw, who lives behind the store, was up late. When he saw a car park in the alley between his house and the store, he watched the occupants sit and smoke. When one got out and tied a bandanna around his face, Sonny dialed 911. Police officers arrived just in time, and eventually the perpetrators were indicted for a string of robberies.

Since then, when I go to work, I know I'm surrounded by what I call "everyday angels." Like the man and his daughter who warned me of trouble. Like Sonny Fondaw, and the 911 operator who acted on his call. And even the round-the-clock customers, who give me a quick hello as they dash in and out for a cup of coffee or a bag of ice. That Tuesday night, I discovered that God uses "everyday angels" to look out for us—and, now and then, some extraordinary ones too.

Looking for the Perfect Present

by Nancy Borghese

*I*n the ten years since my husband, Michael, and I decided to become foster parents, we've offered shelter to many children—some for a brief while, others for as long as a year. One will live in our hearts forever.

We welcomed a curly-haired two-year-old into our home in Massachusetts. Josie* had sparkling brown eyes and a chubby-cheeked smile. She fit right in with our own children, nine-year-old Mikey and twelve-year-old Liz, and soon it felt as if she'd always been part of our family. Josie loved to climb into a laundry basket and shout "Choo choo choo" while Mikey and Liz laughed and pushed her across the floor. One evening as Josie cuddled in my lap, singing softly to herself, I saw Michael look knowingly at me. He could read my thoughts: *This is a child I don't want to give up.*

Josie's mother was addicted to drugs and unable to care for a baby. Josie had some of the problems we'd seen in other children who had suffered abuse or neglect, but during the next two years with us she grew to be a happy, active youngster. Her mother never visited and eventually dropped from sight. Michael and I knew it was just a matter of time before the state would legally release Josie for permanent adoption.

We thought and prayed about what we would do. Michael and I had been Josie's parents for two years. With other children I'd learned to say good-bye, trusting them to God's care. But with Josie it was different. It would break my heart to let her go.

"God's will be done," Michael said, putting his arm around me. He loved Josie as much as I did, but he reminded me we couldn't even

* Name has been changed.

consider keeping her unless the state didn't find any relatives who wanted to adopt her.

Early in its search the Department of Social Services located a cousin who lived in the South. She and her husband were in their thirties. They weren't able to have children, and they wanted Josie. I could find no words for my disappointment, only prayer. "Dear God," I asked, "let them be good people who will love and care for her always."

When Maria* and Charles* arrived in town, we invited them to our house. "It would be more comfortable for Josie than meeting at your hotel," I said on the phone.

"Oh, yes," answered Maria without hesitation. "I agree." My doubts eased a little. She and Charles were putting Josie's well-being first.

I was nervous the day they were to arrive. I straightened the chairs in the living room, fluffed pillows, made sure Josie's hair was combed. But when the doorbell rang and I saw Josie's new parents beaming at the front door, I relaxed. The first thing Charles did was sit down on the floor and play with his daughter-to-be. *He knows kids*, I thought. *Josie will be all right with them.* But still I was hoping for some reassurance that this was what God had planned.

As the day approached for Maria and Charles to take Josie home, I tried to think of a present for them. I wanted it to be special, as special as Josie had been to me. Nothing came to mind, so I went to my favorite shop, asking God to direct me to the perfect gift.

Looking around, I heard from across the store a music box playing "Jesus Loves Me." Josie had just learned that song. *That's exactly what I'm looking for,* I decided. I hurried over, only to discover the music box had been sold to someone else. It was the last in stock.

Discouraged, I wandered through the store, leafing through books, examining ceramic figurines, my thoughts on Josie. *After tomorrow I'll never see her again.* Finally, a framed picture caught my eye, the well-known painting of a guardian angel watching over two children on a bridge. The painting was too familiar to seem special, but there wasn't time to find something else.

* Names have been changed.

The next day Maria and Charles sat on our couch with Josie snuggled between them as Maria started unwrapping my present. When she lifted the painting from the tissue paper, she caught her breath. She looked at me and began to cry.

"Maria, I'm so sorry," I said. "You don't like it."

"Oh, yes, I do," she responded, wiping away the tears. "I love it. How did you know?" I could only stare at her, bewildered.

"In our family it's a tradition," Maria explained. "Each new mother receives this guardian angel picture when her first child is born. Because Charles and I couldn't have kids, I never dreamed anything like this would happen."

The perfect gift. God's answer to prayer, reassuring me that He would keep an eye on Josie.

Angel of God, my guardian dear,
to whom God's love commits me here,
ever this day be at my side
to light and guard,
to rule and guide.

~ Traditional Prayer

UMULT

"Wondrous Sovereign of the sea, Jesus, Savior, pilot me." To hymn
writer Edward Hopper, the storms and strong currents of the sea repre-
sented turbulence in one's life. Even in churning waters, God's guiding
hand was at work.

The following stories illustrate the mysterious ways God can use to
pilot rescuers of people physically threatened by deep waters—a father
and son capsized in the icy depths of Lake Michigan and a toddler nearly
lost in the mighty Mississippi River.

Wreck of the Orysia

by Dan Kulchytsky

ook, Dad!" I pointed to a pair of elegant white swans swimming in the harbor. In more than twenty-five years of sailing
Lake Michigan, we'd seen ducks, geese and thousands of albatross—
but never swans. We couldn't take our eyes off them. Their grace and
beauty were mesmerizing, and they shimmered luminously in the
high afternoon sun of an autumn day. Dad and I were on Washington Island, off the shore of eastern Wisconsin, preparing our
seventeen-foot sloop *Orysia* for a short cruise around Rock Island,
just to the northeast.

We watched the swans a few minutes longer and then got under
way, leaving the harbor about one o'clock with everything shipshape.
The wind was moderate, and *Orysia* cut cleanly through the waves
as I handled the tiller. "We could make it all the way across the lake
on a day like this," Dad said, smiling. Lake Michigan is more than a
hundred miles wide.

We rounded the top of Rock Island from the west, sailing right on course. Heading south, Dad called, "The winds are shifting. We'll have to tack." The smooth lake surface was soon as rough as a washboard. The temperature fell rapidly. *Orysia*'s sails snapped like whips. Around three o'clock, when we finally cleared the eastern side, reaching the passage between Rock and Washington islands, the wind had become fierce. It angled off the cliffs, blowing the water into powerful whirlpools.

"Get her into the wind!" Dad shouted. "I'll get the jib and mainsail down!"

"I'll start the motor," I yelled.

But the wind and current were too strong. Our little boat shuddered, listing to port. With a lurch and a splash of foam, the top of the mast hit the water. We were hurled against the gunwales.

"Hold on!" I cried. Too late! Dad and I were catapulted into the lake, and *Orysia*, with a final heave, capsized, her proud sails plunging into the water.

I grasped the boat's hull, trying to keep myself afloat. The water was so cold it hurt to the bone. "Dad?" I called, looking around frantically. I felt a tug at my sleeve, and Dad surfaced beside me, gasping for air. I pulled myself up on the hull and reached for him. We flopped onto the boat, clutching the keel and shivering violently, our sodden clothing clinging to us. Then a wave surged against the boat and threw me off. "Dad!"

Holding fast to the keel with one hand, my father thrust out his other toward me. Churning waves buffeted *Orysia*, and Dad lost his grip. He slid back into the freezing water, pulling me down with him. We clawed our way back up until we were able to grab on to the boat's keel again.

The winds drove us out into the huge twenty-thousand-square-mile lake. The boat was sinking. Less than a foot of it remained above the surface. Waves crashed over us as we drifted farther from land. Then, below us, we felt the mast smash against a rocky shoal. The impact tossed us back into the water. We could only watch in horror as *Orysia*'s keel disappeared into its housing beneath the waves.

A small part of the hull was still above water, but how would we hold on? Swimming to shore through the turbulent waves was an impossibility. I was almost ready to give up, almost ready to sink into the lake along with the keel. But then I felt Dad's arm around me. He pushed me toward *Orysia*. We both grabbed on and scrambled up, gripping with numb fingers the slot in the hull where the keel had been. Our bodies curved against the bulbous surface, more in the freezing water than out. We hadn't seen any other boats since we had entered the passage, and none would venture forth now in howling winds. *There is no hope for us,* I thought, looking at Dad.

As night fell we turned to prayer. Together and separately, aloud and silently, Dad and I asked that our lives be spared, that God would send help. When the moon rose I was able to see my watch: eight o'-clock. We'd been in the lake for five hours. We talked, trying to keep alert, but our speech became slurred. I knew that meant one thing: Deadly hypothermia was setting in. I'd been cold for so long I began to have feelings of warmth. "Keep moving," Dad urged. We tried shifting our arms, shaking our legs, anything to keep our circulation going.

The full moon cast an eerie glow on the pitching waters. I checked my watch again. Nearly midnight. Nine hours. Our prayers for rescue changed to prayers for mercy. "Thy will be done," Dad said. Death seemed imminent.

Suddenly we heard whirring above us. A searchlight cut through the blackness, reflecting off the waves. A helicopter! "Here!" I shouted, with the little strength I had left. "Here!" Dad echoed, even more weakly than I. We both shouted again, but the roar of the helicopter smothered our cries. The searchlight moved to our right, then to our left, but never shone on us. Abruptly the chopper flew off. *The lake is so big. How will they ever see us? We're two specks down here.*

The helicopter made another pass. We yelled with everything we had left. It flew on, returning several times until I couldn't yell anymore. Dad and I were exhausted. The boat had sunk lower, and we had to lift our heads out of the water just to breathe.

Then I became aware of something to the north of us. I strained to see. I saw white wings. A mirage? No, it was swans! Two swans, just as we'd seen that afternoon in the harbor—floating on the waves in the moonlight, their long necks swaying in a mysterious dance. What were they doing way out here?

"Dad!" My father raised his head. The swans were so beautiful we almost forgot our predicament, and as we watched I saw another searchlight sweeping toward us. A boat! But our hopes plummeted when the light shone away from us. Dad lowered his head, sighing deeply. "No!" I screamed. Almost as if I had been heard, the light swung in our direction again. "Look," I said, helping my father lift his head. "They're coming back!" The powerful beam shot out from the boat's bridge, surrounding us in its glow. We'd been found. Quickly we were hauled on board.

"We were going to head the other way," the fishing tug's skipper told us. "Then we thought we saw two swans in the light." When they looked again, the swans were gone, and they spotted Dad and me instead. The two of us knew the swans *had* been there on the storm-tossed lake, guided by a merciful force greater than nature itself.

A Luminous Dress

by Pam S. Prier

ell, sweetie, think we'll have us a fish fry tomorrow?" I asked, bouncing two-year-old Kira on my lap that steamy July evening. From our vantage point at the top of the steep, rocky riverbank at Ste. Genevieve, Missouri, I saw my fiancé, Shelby, and sons Jesse, nine, and Seanee, six, cast their lines into the Mississippi again. Though they hadn't caught but a few fish all day, I knew from their laughter they were enjoying themselves. I was content to watch from a distance. I wasn't a strong swimmer, and the river's roiling current and muddy brown depths made me uneasy.

"Hey, y'all," Shelby hollered. "Jesse's hooked a big one!"

"C'mon, Jesse, reel it in!" I called.

Kira clapped her hands and giggled. Jesse's T-shirt darkened with sweat as he fought with the fish in humidity so thick you could practically see water droplets hanging in the air.

"I feel hot, Mommy," Kira complained.

"Okay, Baby," I said. I peeled off her clothes. She'd be more comfortable in just her diaper. "Better?"

Evening shaded into night as Jesse struggled with his catch. I was about to tell him to cut the line when I heard him groan in disgust. Soon the guys trudged up, Shelby bringing up the rear, taking it easy because of his heart condition. "The line snapped," Jesse told me. "I almost had it."

"You'll get one next time," I said. He flashed me a smile.

When we packed up our things and loaded them into the car, I realized Kira's favorite sipper cup was missing. *It must have tumbled down the riverbank.* I didn't want Kira to follow me and hurt herself on the rocks while I went to look for it, so I set her in the front seat.

"Stay here, Kira," I said. "I'll be right back." I started down to the water, the boys trailing behind me.

Shelby flipped on the headlights so we could see better, and then joined our search. We were combing the rocks when I heard a loud crunching. I looked up. The car was rolling down the riverbank! Kira!

"Watch out!" I screamed to Jesse. Shoving him out of the car's path, I threw myself against the grille and pushed with all my might. But my slight frame was no match for the downhill momentum of two tons of steel. I leapt out of the way just before it hit the water.

The taillights dipped below the surface. For a moment I was paralyzed in horror. Kira watched me through the open window. The current was already sweeping the car downstream as it filled with water. *No*, I thought, *this isn't good-bye!* I dove in. Shelby jumped in after me, and we struck out for the car, swimming as hard as we could.

"Pam, my boots are weighing me down," Shelby shouted from behind me.

"Kick 'em off," I yelled. I slipped out of my shoes easily, but he was having a tough time with his heavy work boots.

"I'm sorry," Shelby gasped. "I can't go any farther. My heart."

Now I was Kira's only hope of escaping that death trap. "Give me strength," I whispered. With everything I had in me, I focused on my little girl and the car that was carrying her out of my reach.

In the darkness I could barely make out my own arms moving through the water. But somehow I could see Kira up ahead. All around her the air shimmered softly, as if she were standing at my bedroom door in the circle of light cast by the hall lamp, calling for me after a bad dream. With that hazy glow surrounding her, I managed to keep sight of her downstream.

"Mommy?" I could hear Kira's voice trembling as I neared the car. The water washed over the door handles, threatening to flood the front seat where she sat. "I'm here, Baby!" She started climbing out the window.

"No, Kira!" I yelled. "Stay there. Mommy's coming." I lunged desperately for the car. Clutching the door handle in one hand, I reached for Kira with the other.

Instead of her wiggly little body, my fingers grabbed hold of some sort of fabric. I was able to get a good, firm grip on it. As I pulled Kira close, I realized she was wearing a loose, summery dress. It was such a pure white it was almost luminous. What was she doing in a dress?

I didn't have time to ponder the mystery. The car was almost fully submerged, and I couldn't risk its taking us down when it sank to the bottom of the river. I moved away from the doorframe and wearily treaded water. I wouldn't be able to stay afloat much longer, especially with Kira clinging to my neck for all she was worth.

Voices came from on the river. A fishing boat! I swam toward it. "Help! Somebody take my baby!" I cried. "I don't think I can make it."

"She has a baby with her," someone on the boat said. "Randy, you've got to get in there!"

There was a splash, and less than a minute later a man's strong arms were supporting us. "Rest," he said, taking Kira. "I've got her. My friends will swing the boat around and pick us up." When I had caught my breath, he passed Kira back to me. We took turns holding her while we waited, struggling to keep her head above the surface.

But a new danger found us before the man's friends could. The massive hull of a moored river barge loomed above us. In seconds the current would sweep us into it. The man disappeared beneath the surface. I took a deep breath, covered Kira's nose and mouth, and dove under the barge. Praying she would hold her breath, I took my hand away from Kira's face and stroked for the surface, only to bang my head against the bottom of the barge. Frantically I pushed away from it.

Breaking the surface at last, I gulped fresh air. I could hardly hold my head above water. I didn't have any energy left to fight the pull of the depths. Desperately I looked around for the man who'd jumped in to help us. My gaze went toward shore, my thoughts toward my fiancé and my boys there. *I want to come back to you, but I'm not leaving this river without my baby.*

I looked down at Kira's sweet face. She wasn't breathing! "Kira!" I wailed. Then the man was in front of me again, lifting Kira out of my arms and clearing her airway. There was a choking cough before she broke into sobs. I had never thought I would be so glad to hear her cry.

The next thing I knew, the man's friends had reached us. They pulled us aboard their boat and took us to shore. Rescue workers rushed us to an ambulance. "Where's Shelby?" I asked dazedly.

"I'm here," he said, squeezing my hand.

The emergency room doctors examined Kira and me. We were shaken, but otherwise fine. It wasn't until we got home that I remembered the mysterious white dress. "What happened to Kira's dress?" I asked Shelby and a family friend, Grandma Pat. Shelby looked at me strangely. "What dress?" he asked.

I told them what I'd seen when I pulled her out of the sinking car. "It was bright white. You couldn't have missed it."

"Well, she was wearing only a diaper by the time those folks brought you to shore," he said.

"That dress was real," I insisted. "I touched it. I held on to it. God knows I wouldn't have gotten a grip on Kira otherwise."

"Maybe He's the one who put it on her," Grandma Pat offered. "Maybe He had one of His angels lend her a dress so you could see her in the dark and grab hold of her in the water." Chances were better than maybe. The man who'd jumped in to save us told me later that a flash of white had guided him to us. The dress!

Who gave Kira that dress when she had been wearing only a diaper? Who gave me strength to swim to her? Who sent someone to us when we were floundering in the Mississippi? I hadn't been my little girl's only hope then, and I never will be—not with God and His angels around.

NEMPLOYED

"Out of work." If you've ever used the phrase to describe yourself, you know the feelings it draws to the surface. Self-doubt, depression, even despondency. But through a difficult season of unemployment, Rhonda Linn McCloud and a man named Ed received angelic messages of hope that drew them out of despair and ultimately back to work. Let their stories encourage your own walk of faith.

Love and Forgiveness

by Rhonda Linn McCloud

One winter night the confrontation that had been brewing for months finally erupted. When I heard my fourteen-year-old daughter stumble into our apartment past curfew again, I summoned her to my bedroom. "I love you, Kellee," I said, "but I've had it. This behavior can't go on."

She lifted her chin defiantly. How had my innocent daughter turned into a wayward teenager? I could see the sweet, vulnerable little girl inside her, but I just didn't know how to reach her anymore.

Kellee and I had moved to Huntington Beach, California, in the middle of the previous semester, and adjusting to a new school was hard for her. So I looked the other way at first when I found her hanging out with a bunch of older kids whose top priority seemed to be having a good time. Kellee had never taken her studies as seriously as I, a former teacher, would have liked. *At least she's making friends,* I tried to reassure myself.

Then she started coming home at all hours, her eyes glazed, her breath foggy with alcohol. "I'm disappointed in you," I'd harangue her. "I have high expectations for you, and I know you can live up to them." Kellee didn't listen. If anything, her behavior got worse.

That February night I'd had all I could stand. "I won't have you drinking and taking drugs," I said firmly. "Not while you live under my roof. If you stay here, you live by my rules."

"Fine," Kellee snapped. "I'll leave, then. You won't have to worry about me anymore."

"I'll never stop worrying about you," I protested. "I'm your mother." Not saying a word, Kellee snatched her purse and walked out. "The door's always open . . ." I called after her feebly. I was pretty sure she was just going to stay with a girlfriend for a couple nights. Still, a terrible fear crept into my thoughts. What if Kellee had walked not just out of our apartment, but out of my life altogether?

I sank down on my bed, more discouraged than I had ever been. My fiancé had broken off our engagement recently, a blow that hurt almost as much as my divorce from Kellee's dad. Now my daughter was gone too. For as long as I could remember, I had pictured myself as a wife and mother. I'd failed miserably on both counts. *What do I have left to offer?* I wondered. Despair swept over me, and I gave in to it, sobbing so hard it ached to breathe.

Finally, drained, I got up to try to pull myself together. But when I saw my reflection in the bathroom mirror, the hopelessness of my situation struck me anew. Not only had I been unable to handle the all-important responsibilities of wife and mom, I couldn't even find a job to give me the smallest sense of accomplishment. No employer would hire me looking the way I did, and I couldn't blame any of them.

My face was covered with ugly blisters, the result of osteomyelitis, a type of bone infection. It had started after a minor accident during a root canal nine years earlier. The tip of a metal file had broken off and lodged in the root of my tooth, causing an infection in my jawbone that had failed to respond to treatment and had spread to other parts of my body. Now my appearance frightened even me.

I turned away from the mirror. Back in my bedroom I paused at the window. Gazing out into the starry night, I started praying. *God,* I pleaded, picturing Him wrapping a deep-purple blanket around Kellee to keep her safe, *please protect my daughter.* I knew it was up to Him now. *And please help me find peace in my life.*

I lay down again. The last thing I saw before I closed my eyes was the electric treetop angel I'd saved from Christmas and hung above my bed. The soft glow of its lights always brought me comfort, comfort I desperately needed that night. *God, release me from my pain. What's the point of going on? Everyone I love leaves me.*

I hadn't been asleep long when I found myself getting out of bed. I walked out the front door and stood on the balcony, looking at the sky, a canopy of midnight blue. Then, amazingly, I was floating over the balcony railing, up into the velvet expanse. I realized I must be dreaming, but I felt fully awake.

The stars were so near that I couldn't resist touching them. Their texture felt like snow melting in my hands. I peered more closely at them. All around me, as far as my eyes could see, were tiny angels! Garbed in a glistening crystalline substance so they looked like snowflakes, they whispered past me, drifting somewhere on the breeze.

The next thing I knew I had glided to a stop in a cloud. Someone was standing beside me, and I glanced over to see who it was. Love, pure and boundless, streamed from Him, suffusing me with a cosmic sense of well-being immediately. I knew I was in the presence of Christ. And I knew He was directing the angels—to earth, to do His work.

Gently He wrapped his left arm around my shoulders and held me close to Him. Neither of us spoke, yet communication flowed between us. *I am your brother,* He told me. *And I will always be with you.*

I nodded. I know that now, but I need to know one thing more. What is my purpose on earth?

His answer was unhesitating: *To give and receive love; to give and receive forgiveness.*

"Love and forgiveness." Those words were on my lips when I woke, rested and renewed. But whom did I love? Whom did I need to forgive?

In the days following I began to make a list. I prayed over every name during the next months. My ex-husband, Kellee's father, for our failed marriage. I'd had my part in it too. My dentist, for causing the infection in my jawbone during that root canal. It was an unfortunate accident and I knew he felt badly. My former fiancé, for ending our relationship. It wouldn't have been right for either of us. Slowly I let go of my anger and hurt.

But what about Kellee? Six months later she still hadn't come home. Technically she wasn't a runaway. She sporadically checked in with my mother to say she was okay. But Kellee didn't want to speak to me. Though I longed to talk with her, I had to accept that she wasn't ready to reestablish our relationship. The longer she stayed away, the more I came to accept that she was her own person. *I forgive you for not being the serious student I wanted you to be,* I told her in my thoughts. *I love you the way you are: bright, creative, free-spirited. I hope you'll forgive me. I only wanted to protect you.*

I could feel my emotional wounds beginning to heal. With the help of prayer, the problems that used to drive me into despair gradually became bearable.

Yet somehow I didn't feel completely free of the pain of my past. *Do I still harbor negative feelings toward someone that I need to get over?* I wondered.

One morning as I gave myself the usual cursory once-over in the mirror, I noticed the blisters on my face weren't as inflamed. My skin looked as if it was getting better! Marveling at how my illness seemed to be abating, I gave thanks to God.

Almost like an answer, the words Christ had communicated to me in my dream came back. *Love and forgiveness.* Gazing at my reflection, I knew what I had to do before I could be whole again. It was going to be a long, complicated process, but I needed to learn to love and forgive myself.

It helped when Kellee finally came home nine months after she had left. "I love you, Mom," she said. "I want to try again. Will you give me another chance?"

"If you'll do the same for me," I replied. I hugged my daughter tight, and I didn't think anything could feel better.

When Kellee told me she had started going to a twelve-step recovery program to help deal with her drinking and drug abuse, I was proud of her. I was grateful. I knew God had sent His angels to watch over Kellee when I couldn't.

Now it was time to find something to give me a sense of purpose.

I thought of counseling over the telephone, where people wouldn't be put off by my appearance and where my education in behavioral science and my experiences in life might be of use.

I contacted mental-health programs in the area, and New Hope, a suicide and crisis hot line, had an opening for a counselor. When I saw the title of the manual I received on the first day of training, I knew I had found the right place. "Giving Life by Giving Love."

Not long after that I was led to a doctor who was able to treat my osteomyelitis successfully, and eventually the infection in my jawbone cleared up completely. My appearance returned to normal.

Love and forgiveness. They have brought me a release from my pain far beyond what I could have ever imagined. As my faith in myself has grown, so have my job and my relationship with my daughter. At New Hope, I train new counselors. I also teach parenting classes in Huntington Beach. Under my guidance Kellee studied at home and earned her high-school-equivalency certificate. She is now a student at a local college. Today, four years after that desperate winter night when I nearly gave up all hope, God's blessings continue—carried into my life, I like to think, on the snowy wings of His angels.

"Do You Want Help?"

by John Powers

No matter which direction I walked on the night of December 23, thirty years ago, the sleet found a place to stick to my blue uniform. It was the type of night a foot patrolman wonders why he became a cop. I was doing security checks in an industrial park in South Jamaica, Queens. Every business in this remote area had been closed for hours, and there wasn't another human being for blocks as I made my rounds throughout the eerily quiet complex.

By nine the wind and frigid weather had intensified, and I took shelter under a large canopy, clicking my heels together to get the blood moving in my feet. Finally my sergeant came by and told me to stay where I was until my shift was over. As the squad car pulled off, I felt uneasy about being alone in such a deserted place. *Stay alert, Powers,* I told myself. *Don't get spooked.* Then I heard footsteps. I braced my hand on the gun in my holster and swung around at the ready.

"Sorry, Officer, I didn't mean to startle you."

White male, fair-skinned, five-foot-ten, one hundred seventy pounds, I noted, my training kicking in. *Late fifties, early sixties, wears his age well.*

"The name's Ed."

I removed my hand from my gun. "Officer Powers," I introduced myself, deciding the guy was harmless. "I'm on patrol."

Ed said his sympathy went out to me, working outdoors in this weather. "And at Christmastime, no less," he said. "There was a time in my life when I was caught out in the cold. It was a night very similar to this."

I could tell this was the beginning of a long story and that this guy was going to talk until he finished telling it, but I was glad to have the company and settled in to listen.

"Thirty-five years ago, on Christmas Eve morning," Ed began, "I crawled out of the cardboard box I called home on the Bowery. Hung over and half frozen, I looked up through the falling snow at the Manhattan Bridge, hanging in midair like a ghost. By the time I hit Canal Street, I was shivering, my mind slipping in and out of focus. But I had plans: This would be the day I was going to end my life. The looming iron ghost was the answer. I would jump in front of a truck coming off the bridge. *A semitrailer,* I thought, *that will do the job.*"

So on Christmas Eve in the 1930s, in the depths of alcoholic despair, Ed waited at the foot of the Manhattan Bridge. The only thing keeping him standing was knowing that any minute his misery would be over. During the several hours he stood there, however, not a single truck came off that bridge.

"When I could no longer bear my hunger, I decided to try my luck at panhandling, for old-time's sake," Ed grinned.

Back on Canal Street the first person he asked turned away disgusted. The next person he asked was a distinguished-looking young man of thirty or so. He wore a lovely tan overcoat, dress shoes and no hat, which Ed thought odd. "Sir, could you help me get a cup of coffee?" Ed asked.

The young man glanced around. "Follow me," he said, gesturing toward a diner. There he invited Ed to take a seat at the counter and ordered him coffee and a deluxe breakfast. "A meal I'll never forget," Ed said. Before paying the bill, the young man asked the waitress to add a hot roast beef sandwich and coffee to go. Ed was amazed by the stranger's generosity, and for a time he was distracted from his desperate plan. "A warm lunch tucked into my coat pocket," Ed said, "I went back to the alley where I'd spent the night, dozed for a while, then ate when I awoke. My stomach was full, but my situation was still bleak. What did I have to live for? Determined to see my plan through, I returned to the bridge."

Ed waited again, until afternoon became evening. Still not a truck in sight. "God, I do not want to live another night. Please help me," he prayed, not knowing the bridge had been closed to truck traffic due to fierce weather conditions.

Maybe because it was the only thing he knew how to do, maybe

out of habit, Ed went back to panhandling on Canal Street. The few people he came across had their own challenges in this brutal weather, trying to get home to their families for Christmas Eve.

In his stupor Ed at first didn't recognize one of the people he approached. "The young man looked me in the eye and said, 'Do you want help?' At that moment I felt a blazing warmth throughout my body. Something in my life had changed."

Once again the young man led Ed into the diner they had visited that morning. He ordered a hot open-faced turkey sandwich and all the traditional holiday side dishes. While Ed ate, the young man excused himself, returning to the diner in about fifteen minutes without a hint that he'd been out in the storm. In fact, Ed never noticed a single flake or wet spot marring the dapper tan overcoat or fancy dress shoes.

"We must hurry," the young man said, putting away his wallet and jostling Ed out the door. "We have an appointment with a friend of mine."

The young man led Ed at a fast pace to a building a few blocks away, where a sign advertised Day Employment. Inside, the young man's friend said a two-week job was available, if Ed was interested, for a watchman at a warehouse in Queens. Ed nodded at the young man, who said to his friend, "Make the arrangements. We'll be right back."

Now the young man hurried Ed to an Army-Navy store, where he consulted Ed about his size and bought a warm winter jacket, two sets of khaki pants and shirts, work boots, underwear, long johns, socks and a woolen watch cap. Ed was flabbergasted and somewhat embarrassed as they rushed back to the employment office with the packages. "Right in the bathroom of the employment agency, I put on a complete new outfit from head to toe," Ed said. "Wonderful, warm, dry clothes."

Before leaving the building, the young man gave Ed subway and bus directions to the Queens warehouse—and a five-dollar bill. Finally Ed asked his name: Jim. "How will I ever repay you, Jim?" Ed wanted to know.

The young man put his hand on Ed's shoulder. "If you stay off the street and don't abuse your body with liquor, that will be my payment."

Together they walked to the subway station, where the two men parted ways. "Merry Christmas," Jim said. Ed waved good-bye as he descended the stairs with his packages.

After an hour-and-a-half trip, Ed arrived at the warehouse in Queens, where he found the owner's son, Phil, waiting for him with open arms. "My whole family is grateful to have you here," Phil said. They went over the arrangement—two weeks at the warehouse day and night, a cot to sleep on and takeout food nearby. After giving Ed a few more instructions and an advance in salary, Phil was on his way.

"And that's how I came to be in my own warehouse," Ed explained, "secure and warm on Christmas Eve, when only a few hours earlier I wanted the final curtain to ring down. I owed my life to Jim, and I thanked God for putting him in my path, not once but twice."

Ed didn't think he could be any happier. But then on Christmas Day a car pulled up at the warehouse, and in walked Phil and his family. Phil introduced his wife and their two daughters, who set up a turkey dinner with all the trimmings for Ed. Then they handed him a present wrapped in holiday paper. When Ed opened it and found a beautiful brown cable-knit sweater, he put it to his face to smell the freshness of the wool. He couldn't believe his good fortune.

During his two-week stint, Ed made a point of getting to know all the employees. When Phil offered him the job full time, Ed jumped at the chance. "It's settled, then," Phil said. "Follow me." And they walked to a plywood-framed structure at the rear of the plant.

Here in the story, Ed stopped abruptly. "Why, pardon me, Officer Powers," he said, "you've been in the cold long enough." I'd honestly forgotten about the weather, and the time, and a glance at my watch verified that my shift was over. "Step inside for just a moment," Ed said. "It will be the perfect end to my story."

I followed Ed to the plywood structure, just as he had followed Phil some thirty-five years before. Ed opened the door and the lights went on.

"Come in, come in," he said. And I entered a comfortable three-

room apartment, complete with all the amenities and wallpapered to match the decor. "I've lived here ever since," Ed explained. "The owner's family and the employees never forget me on a holiday, and they always remember that I consider Christmas Eve my birthday, the day Jim saved my life and I was reborn.

"One more thing," Ed said. "I eventually sent some money to Jim, in care of his friend at the agency. I wanted him to know how well things had turned out for me. But the money came back with a note. A man at the agency remembered me well, but he knew of no Jim. You see, no one had been with me at the agency that Christmas Eve. No one visible, that is."

I left Ed with a new spring in my step. His story carried me through many a hard tour on the force. I had met someone whose life was completely changed thanks to the goodness in this world and to God's abundant goodness, which rains on us from heaven.

ACATION

Vacation. It's an opportunity to "get away" from the daily routine. But does it mean we "get away" from God and His watchful care? No. Even in our leisure—at the rim of the Grand Canyon, in a beach hotel, on an isolated desert island—God and His messengers are near.

Unlikely Visitors

by Jan Smith

We were both born-and-bred Texans, but in 1964 my husband, Howard, and I were thinking of moving somewhere else. Howard was just out of the Marines, and in June we visited some of his old buddies in northern California while we looked for work there. You could say things were up in the air with us. When we finally headed back to Texas, nothing had been decided about our future, and I was feeling down.

Checking the road map as we crossed into Nevada, I had an idea. "How about some fun?" I asked. "We could see the Grand Canyon." We would have to turn north and go out of our way, but Howard's face brightened. "Let's go!" he said.

We'd always wanted to visit the Grand Canyon, often poring over pictures of it at home and dreaming of a trip. But pictures and dreams can't begin to prepare you for the real thing. I couldn't believe my eyes when we first entered the park. *God's creation in all its wonder,* I thought, as we stared across the boundless space from the canyon's rim.

The weather was warm, and I was glad I'd worn only my favorite red shorts and a cool shirt. We opened the windows wide to catch the breeze as we drove along the park's southern edge. About every fifteen minutes I called, "Stop here!" and jumped out of the car to take a picture. My clothes and white tennis shoes were soon brown with dust, but I didn't care.

I was almost out of film by the time we reached the northwestern corner of the canyon. "One last picture!" I begged, spotting a beautiful lookout point below a thick hedge just off the road. Howard pulled over and I leapt from the car. I ran behind the hedge and down three steps toward a landing enclosed by an iron guard rail. As I stepped onto the landing with my right foot, the rubber sole of my shoe crunched on a thick layer of pea-sized gravel. Holding tight to the camera around my neck, I tried to regain my balance, but my foot flew out from under me. I fell on my back, my legs in the air, and began to slide across the gravel. The landing sloped at a forty-five-degree angle, and I couldn't stop myself. I was heading feet first toward the canyon's waiting mouth.

Grab the guard rail! I reached for the lower iron bar of the rail— but missed. I was so skinny I went right under it. The camera swung wildly and smashed against the canyon wall, film unspooling into the wind, the cord pressing at my neck. I felt my head leave the edge of the landing. Scrub brush growing from the canyon wall tore at me as I slid downward. All I could see was sky above and the open canyon below. I stretched my arms high over my head, reaching up—hoping, praying, trying to stop myself from sliding. I was grabbing at the air! *If I could only find something to hold on to . . .*

A hand! Someone caught my wrist in a powerful grip, instantly stopping my slide down the wall. There was no struggle, no jerk of my body. My shoulders and back pressed against the rock.

"Are you okay, my dear?" asked a tall old man with white hair. He had soft eyes and a healthy glow to his face. He smiled a grandfatherly smile, and I knew I could trust him with my life. "Up we go," he said. And with one swift movement I was lifted out of the canyon and laid safely on the gravel landing. *How could anyone so old be so strong?*

Catching my breath, I looked more closely at my rescuer. The man was probably in his seventies. His clothes were old-fashioned and carefully pressed. I admired his stiff white shirt with a tall collar and wide tie. His polished black shoes were long and narrow and laced up with neatly tied bows. Stooping beside him was an old woman, looking at me with twinkling dark eyes. She wore a long print dress, tight around her neck with a lace collar draped in a semicircle down to her ample bosom. There was a cameo at the center of her throat. Her hose were thick and black, her high-top shoes shiny with a wide heel. The man and woman were picture-perfect, not a speck of dust on either of them.

The woman enfolded me in her arms. She and her companion helped me to my feet, cooing over me, trying to soothe me. They straightened my clothes and took the broken camera from my neck. When I calmed down, they moved to either side of me and we walked up the steps and around the hedge. Howard was waiting patiently in the car. Only a few minutes had elapsed. He knew nothing of what had happened until he saw me.

I winced as Howard put me in the car. "You'll find help for her there," the man said, pointing up the road to the left. "It's a hospital," added the woman.

"Thank you!" Howard said, closing my door and hurrying behind the wheel. "Thank you," I called as strongly as I could. We turned to wave at the elderly couple as we drove away. They walked toward the landing and disappeared behind the hedge.

"Where did they go?" Howard asked. "Where did they come from?" I countered. Two old people dressed in some kind of outdated Sunday best—unlikely clothes for canyon visitors. And the man couldn't have been standing on the ledge when he grabbed my wrist. I'd slid too far to be reached from there. Had he been climbing around the steep walls of the canyon? Impossible!

The hospital was just where the couple told us it would be. Doctors and attendants treated me, cleaning my wounds, meticulously picking gravel from all over my body. They found scrapes from scrub brush on my head, neck and shoulders. They all shook their heads in disbelief. This was proof to them that I had indeed fallen into the canyon.

Today I see the old couple as clearly in my mind as I did when they stood on either side of me. Back then Howard and I decided the best thing to do was to stay put for the time being. And in the end Texas has always been home. But that doesn't mean I haven't seen other changes in my life. Always, when insecurities leave me up in the air, I remember God's steadying grip.

Master, our Master, oh let it be
That our leisure and rest be still
with Thee,
With Thee and for Thee each
sunny hour.

~ Frances Ridley Havergal

January Roses

by Cathy Lee Phillips

When I lost my husband I lost my companion, my lover, my best friend. Jerry died of complications from a heart transplant; after only six years of marriage, I became a widow at age thirty-five. We should have been laughing and looking forward to a long, happy life together. Instead the years ahead loomed like an endless, deserted highway.

As the initial numbness faded, sadness overwhelmed me. I sank into a depression that deepened with each passing month. Time was supposed to heal all wounds, but for me it was an enemy that carried Jerry further away.

I had a strong faith. Jerry had been a minister, and I was a director of Christian education. Nevertheless, grief and loneliness overshadowed my faith, and the solace I had once found in God was gone.

Occasionally I was able to lose myself in my work or enjoy an evening out with friends, but as soon as I walked through my front door, the silent house reminded me of the emptiness of life without Jerry. I'd look at the piano and think of how he loved to hear me play and sing. The couch in the living room made me remember our evenings snuggled in front of the TV. Some nights I lay awake for hours, missing the warmth of Jerry's body beside me.

Special occasions—Valentine's Day, Jerry's birthday, our anniversary—were the most difficult. Even Thanksgiving and Christmas, with family dinners to distract me, were devoid of joy.

As the first anniversary of Jerry's death grew nearer, I didn't want to think about what I was going to do. Should I pretend it was just another day? Should I spend the day looking through our photo albums, reliving happier times?

Finally I decided the only place I might find peace was the beach. It had always been a place of rest and serenity for me. I wanted to hear and feel the power of God's sea, to inhale the sharp, briny air. Maybe that would make me feel alive again, close to God again.

I made reservations at a hotel on Amelia Island, Florida, where I had stayed once. It seemed an ideal place for solitary reflection and renewal.

On the morning of January 12, I awoke early in my hotel room, my mind flooded with memories of that day one year before. The brown warm-up suit Jerry wore in the hospital—a Christmas gift from me. The afternoon we spent together, sitting side by side on the starchy sheets of his bed, looking through the classifieds for a new puppy to keep me company while he recovered. Later, the emergency call from the hospital. The short drive there, which seemed to take an eternity. The stark words, "We couldn't bring him back."

I knew a walk along the Amelia Island shore would clear my head, so I forced myself to get out of bed. I looked through the window. A wall of thick gray fog had rolled in. The mist obscured everything—the water, the sand, the seagulls, even the hotel courtyard. A walk was out of the question.

Sliding open the glass door, I stepped out onto the balcony and slumped into a deck chair. All I wanted to do was walk on the beach.

I sat there glaring resentfully into the dense fog. Then, in the rhythmic rush of the waves against the shore, I thought I heard a whisper. Or was it the surf?

You can't see the water, but you know it is near.

What? Then I heard the words a second time. *You can't see the water, but you know it is near.*

The words receded and, in that moment of quiet, I understood. I couldn't see the ocean through the fog. But I could smell its saltiness in the air. I could hear the sound of the surf and the cry of the seagulls. Wasn't it the same with God?

A soft knock at the door interrupted my thoughts. I was puzzled; I didn't know anyone on the island. A hotel maid walked in, holding a glass vase with a beautiful bouquet of pale pink roses.

"I thought you might like these," she said, setting the vase on a side table and rearranging the flowers.

I was stunned, and it must have shown on my face because she apologized. "I'm sorry," she said. "I didn't mean to startle you."

"It's not that," I said, unable to stop my tears.

"I found the roses in another part of the hotel," she said. "I can't explain it, but something told me to bring them to this room."

I looked at the bouquet more closely. *That's odd,* I thought. *Not a dozen. Not a half dozen . . .*

Then I told her about Jerry, about my loneliness. As I poured my heart out to this stranger, the fog of pain lifted. "Jerry used to give me pink roses on special occasions," I said. "We would have celebrated our seventh anniversary this year."

The maid hugged me tight. "I know you're still grieving, but life is more than grief," she promised as she slipped out the door.

Standing in the middle of my room, I stared at the bouquet. Seven pink roses. I heard the whisper once more: *You can't see the water, but you know it is near.*

Thank You, God, for telling me Jerry is safe with You, and I must go on. Thank You for the seven pink roses—and for the angel who delivered them.

AR ZONE

A wartime crisis can push the most courageous men and women to their limits. But even there, at the outer edge of human endurance, God makes His presence known—with a message that says, "Have courage. Don't lose heart. Look for the bold peace that I can place inside you, where it counts."

A Face from Above

by Larry Horn

I was nineteen years old in 1968, an Army medic assigned to an aid station near the South Vietnamese hamlet of Tan An. Because of my youth, death and fear had never reached deeply into my experience. That would all change with the Tet Offensive, one of the bloodiest battles of the Vietnam War.

Ordinarily the medical corps was not expected to fight on the battlefield. In previous wars medics had been noncombatants, giving aid at the front to wounded soldiers before they were evacuated to field hospitals. Vietnam was different. The rules broke down. Everyone and everything was a target—even aid stations. Medical corps or not, we were expected to defend our position against the enemy.

For several nights we had been warned of a Vietcong offensive and ordered into a foxhole. Each time turned out to be a false alarm. Once again on the night of February 28 an alert was given. "Horn, Jacobs," our first sergeant said to me and another medic, Bill Jacobs, a good friend, "take up your defensive positions." It was one of the last orders he would ever give, or Bill would ever hear.

We picked up our M-16 rifles and climbed into the foxhole, a five-foot square of earth fortified by sandbags piled four feet high. For ten or fifteen minutes we made small talk to pass the time before the all-clear announcement we knew would come.

Then came a terrifying sound overhead—the telltale whoosh of incoming mortar rounds. All at once the silence of the night was pierced by cries of "Incoming! Incoming!"

The first round pounded the earth a hundred feet from our foxhole. Beads of sweat trickled down my face. Bill and I huddled against the ground as the explosions grew closer. There was another unnerving whoosh. But instead of hearing the burst of an exploding round, I saw a blinding white flash, whiter than anything. All at once I was floating, weightless. Time stopped.

When I came to, I was lying on my back several yards away from the foxhole. The stench of gunpowder mixed with burning flesh clogged my nostrils. I could hear my M-16 popping off rounds from the intense heat of the mortar explosion. Around me the fighting raged on, the sound of mortar fire mixed with the screams of the injured and the moans of the dying.

My mind slowly pieced together my predicament. I had no sensation below my waist. My back rested in a puddle of hot, sticky ooze, which I realized was my blood making mud out of the earth. Blinded by sand and debris, I called upon what I was sure was the last of my courage and allowed my hands to reach below my hips. I felt two jagged objects, like broken tree limbs. With horror I realized they were the thighbones of each leg. My hands quickly retreated to my face, cradling it, as if I were trying to comfort myself the way I might have comforted an injured soldier brought to our aid station.

I lay helplessly in the dark, alone. Shells exploded all around me and smoke thickened the air. My mouth was as dry as powder, and every cell in my body thirsted for water. I shivered uncontrollably. My mind wandered to my family back home in Massachusetts. I wondered if I'd ever see them again, if I'd ever go home again.

Despite my injuries I was in no pain. I grew almost tranquil as I slipped closer to death. But that feeling soon gave way to panic as I sensed the rumble of an approaching tank, one assigned to our station. I was almost directly in its path. What if the crew didn't see me?

I tried to raise a hand and call out, but all effort was useless. Passing a mere ten feet from my head, shaking the earth, the tank churned up the dirt as it got into position. It had just missed me.

The tank fire turned the enemy back, and moments after the guns fell silent a fellow medic was attending to me. Bill was dead. Even through my blurred vision, the look on the medic's face told me I was in real bad shape. In the treatment room drops were put in my eyes. They tried to start two intravenous lines, but couldn't because I had "bled out"—not enough blood was circulating in my arms to keep a vein up. There was nothing to do but load me on a chopper to the Twenty-Fourth Evac Hospital.

The triage room at the Twenty-Fourth was controlled chaos. The enemy had struck several installations that night. Doctors and nurses worked their way through a sea of critically wounded and dying soldiers, identifying the ones who could be saved and starting treatment. The lingering wet smell of blood and gunpowder hung in the room. My pant leg still smoldered. This was truly hell on earth. The medical staff labored intently over me. I watched them frantically cut away what was left of my uniform and apply tourniquets to my shattered legs. Deep within my being I felt a tide of pure hysteria rising, something far beyond ordinary human fear or even panic, something more closely akin to one final desperate effort to fight off death.

At that decisive instant, as I hovered between life and the hereafter, a face appeared above me, the face of a man in his late fifties at least, perhaps early sixties. A universe of calm seemed to exist behind his eyes, and his presence blocked out the misery around me. He pressed a warm, reassuring hand on my shoulder and said in a voice that flowed from him, "You will be all right. They are going to insert IV needles into veins on both sides of your neck. You must remain very, very still." Almost imperceptibly he grasped my head. I barely felt the needles going in. Rather, I concentrated completely on the placid visage before me, my gaze locked into his.

Blood poured into my body—one unit, two, four. With it came life. And pain. I began to thrash uncontrollably, hardly able to withstand the agony in my legs. The stranger's gentle hands continued to hold my head firmly. If the needles infusing blood into me tore open the veins of my neck, all hope was lost.

Suddenly panic overwhelmed me. "I'm going to die! I'm going to die!" I screamed.

"No, you are not going to die," the man said in a calm, soothing tone. "Look at my face. Take slow, steady breaths and look at my face."

I fought desperately against my terror. I didn't take my eyes off his face. The thinly etched wrinkles that furrowed his features made me think of wisdom and strength. His eyes were the color of a perfect spring sky, and just as clear. His hair was gray, with a hint of white, and close-cropped, only about a quarter of an inch at the top. His appearance embodied everything I needed at that moment—protection, reassurance, peace. Even if I had wanted to turn away, I couldn't. Something about him held me utterly in his power.

Finally, after doctors had replaced my entire blood volume twice over, I was prepped for surgery. I didn't know if they would save my life, let alone my legs, but the last words the stranger spoke to me before I went under were, "Son, you will be fine."

And I was. Four days later I awoke in one of the wards at the Twenty-Fourth. I had no feeling from the waist down, so I was considerably relieved when the nurse pulled aside my blankets and I saw my legs, broken, bloodied and bandaged but still there. There was never a prettier sight than my blue and swollen toes. Quickly enough the feeling came back in my legs, and with a vengeance.

I insisted on thanking the man who had stood over me and guided me through triage. The nurses knew of no one who fit the description. They said there wasn't a person older than forty in the whole hospital, and certainly no man with gray or white hair. I asked to see the chaplain, and he agreed to make some inquiries. He returned with the same answer. There was no such person.

"Then whom or what did I see?" I demanded.

"I don't know, Larry, but if you need a name, call it the face of God."

I've thought about that a lot in these years since, and I don't believe I actually came face to face with God. I don't think we are meant to, at least not on earth. But there are beings who travel between heaven and earth. It is in their faces that we can see the face of God.

My True Confession

by Paul Galanti

I was lashed to a wooden stool in an unheated interrogation room at what we American POWs ruefully called the Hanoi Hilton. The ropes binding my hands behind me cut deep into my wrists. On the floor a few feet in front of me was a bowl of watery gruel in a rusted, lopsided tin. This was Day 10 of another period of torture and interrogation.

By then, January 1969, I had been a prisoner of the North Vietnamese for two and a half years, after I was shot down during my ninety-seventh combat mission. After I ejected from my crippled Navy Skyhawk attack bomber, an enemy bullet had caught me in the neck while I dangled helplessly from my parachute. Captured, I had been forced to march for twelve days to the prison in Hanoi. There the process of breaking me down began, as it did for all American POWs, with trying to force me to sign a written confession of my "war crimes." I was brutally beaten and psychologically tortured. Still, like most of my compatriots, I refused to sign.

I eyed the battered tin, as did the rats in the grimy, freezing room. To eat, I had to rock my stool until it fell forward. Then, like a starving animal, I would lap up my one daily ration of gruel, hoping the guard outside wouldn't wait too long before coming in and pulling me upright again, lest the rats eat the dribbles of food off my chin. But this was a respite. Sooner or later another torture session would begin.

Torture could last hours at a time. They used a rope contraption to twist my limbs into pretzellike contortions, tightening the restraints until the agony was beyond unbearable and the only reality was the stupefying pain. When my mind drifted, my captors' shouts and slaps penetrated the haze, bringing me back.

Worse in some ways was the time between interrogations. Dragged back to my dingy cell, I languished in cramped isolation for months. I was forbidden to speak with my fellow prisoners, communicating only sporadically by whispering and surreptitious tapping in code on the walls. The days passed mostly in silence. I spent hours trying to keep myself sane by formulating to the minutest detail all the grand business schemes I planned to carry out after the war. Sometimes I watched what we called Hanoi racing spiders, big furry things that could actually rout the rats and devour the lizards that sped over the rough, clammy walls.

I couldn't take my eyes off the gruel. I knew I needed its paltry nourishment to endure another round of barbarous punishment in the interrogation room, but I could not bring myself to fall over and lap it up. I tried to pray for strength. *Dear Lord . . .*

Even quasireligious types like me turned to prayer regularly in the Hanoi Hilton. I was the son of a highly decorated Army colonel and had attended ecumenical chapels at bases all over the world for most of my life. But faith had never meant much to me. I was more interested in the hard-living, girl-chasing image that fighter pilots cultivated. I toned that down when I married Phyllis, but religion was still pretty much just a Sunday-morning kind of thing for me.

On Sunday mornings at the Hanoi Hilton, though, I at last made a deep connection with faith. None of us could afford to turn his back on God. Three deliberate, commanding thumps on the wall were the signal for all of us to stand for services. Alone in our cells, we said the Lord's Prayer and then the Pledge of Allegiance, our voices mingling in the narrow passageway outside.

Now, awaiting the return of my tormentors and trying to gather an appetite for the cold slop in the dirty pan, I felt I couldn't go on, even with God's help. I was too weak, too broken. I would never sign a confession, but I couldn't endure much more of this agony. What was the sense of eating? I was dying anyway, dying from the inside out, not just from the pain but from the utter senselessness of it. I was at a point where it seemed almost a crime to go on living. I wouldn't eat. I would die instead.

At that instant of spiritual and psychological checkmate, slumped on my stool, I experienced something so powerful that it affects my life to this day. With complete clarity I realized I was not alone in that desolate room. The veil of suffering lifted and I saw clearly a figure standing near me. He wore a white robe more vivid than any earthly garment I have ever seen. Though I could not make out his features,

I could tell he was bearded. Then, in a voice I heard with my whole being, he told me, "Paul, you are going to be all right. I am always with you."

I was still bound but suddenly I felt free, the flames of my despair smothered by comfort and reassurance. Those words, I knew, were the words of Jesus, delivered by an angel. It was Christ alone who had command over life, and He was telling me that with Him all suffering could be endured, all pain soothed.

Suddenly my companion was no longer visible, and I was alone again with my pitiful meal. Yet it beckoned me like a feast. I tipped over the stool and ate gratefully.

That particular go-around with the interrogators lasted two more weeks, and I survived four more years as a captive in the Hanoi Hilton. In 1973 I was finally able to come home and get started on some of those business plans I had dreamed up in my prison cell to pass the long, solitary hours. That day when the angel delivered the words that saved me, I did make a confession—a confession of faith. My life was saved, not just once but forever.

TRAORDINARY

There's nothing commonplace about any of the true stories you've read in this book. But hold on. Here are accounts of two extraordinary manifestations of God's protection in astonishing, perilous circumstances. Are you ready for the ride?

Invisible Protection

by Amanda Proctor*

*L*et me say at the outset that Carl is getting professional help at a domestic-violence treatment center. Because I do not want to hurt his chances of recovery, I have changed names and locations to camouflage his identity. Otherwise I am putting down exactly what happened on the night of May 10, 1994.

Carl Broderick and his wife, Marie, were my landlords and next-door neighbors just outside Lubbock, Texas. We shared a driveway, but that's about all we had in common. I drove a 1987 Plymouth Voyager; Carl drove a brand-new Bronco and his wife a silver Cadillac. Their house was large; mine was small. They liked cats, and I had a dog, a big German shepherd mix named—more hopefully than accurately—Saint.

With so little to draw us together, it came as a surprise that Marie and I hit it off from the moment I moved into their tenant house. Marie helped me unpack, arrange the furniture in the three-room

*Name has been changed.

bungalow and repair a fence around the property to keep Saint off the highway. She also helped me take down the plywood panels the previous renters had used to block most of the windows.

"Why was the house all boarded up?" I asked.

"There goes my phone," Marie said, hurrying off. But her phone hadn't rung. Later I wondered if the tenants had boarded up the house because they were afraid of Carl.

I was in my kitchen, about seven months after moving in, when I heard Carl shouting angrily. Then silence, followed by more shouts. A few minutes later Marie came running across the driveway, her long, graying hair loosened from its combs.

"We had a little argument," she said. She looked as though she'd been crying. I asked if Carl had hit her. "Of course not," she said. I wasn't so sure.

Paul Bailey and Matthew Nelson were Marie's childhood friends, and both were worried about her husband's behavior too—and her safety. Paul, who lived just up the road, was a bantam-sized, take-charge guy who wore a diamond earring in his left ear. Matthew, who lived with his wife in Lubbock, was a gentle, heavyset, long-haul truck driver. I liked both men, even if Saint didn't.

Saint's grudge was with Matthew. Unaccountably, the big guy was afraid of dogs, and dogs can sense attitudes. Anytime Matthew came near our property the hair on Saint's neck rose and he went into a barking frenzy. It was his "Matthew bark"—not the joyful greeting he gave most people, but a low half-bark, half-growl.

On May 10, 1994, around 8:00 P.M.—maybe three weeks after the shouting episode—I was driving home from my job as a medical technician in Lubbock when I was startled to see Marie running down the highway through the semidarkness toward me. I pulled over and Marie scrambled in. Her blouse was torn, her hair was disheveled and there was blood on her face and hands.

"Carl's gone crazy!" she sobbed. "He beat me up and smashed the Cadillac!"

The story tumbled out: Carl was drinking and taking drugs again. When Marie reproached him, he began to push her around. Marie ran outside and got into her Cadillac. Carl came after her. He jerked open the car door, grabbed her by the hair, threw her on the ground, jumped into the car and drove it through the side of the garage. While he struggled to get the dented car door open, Marie ran out to the road. Crouching in the drainage ditch, she'd seen Carl's Bronco roar out of the driveway and turn west.

I wanted to go straight to the police, but Marie didn't want "to get the whole world involved." Instead, she asked me to drive her home; before Carl got back, she'd pack a bag and find a safe place to stay.

Reluctantly, keeping a wary eye out for Carl, I turned into our drive. I could see the rear bumper of the silver Cadillac protruding from the splintered wall of the garage. Marie ran into her house. When she came out carrying an overnight bag, she told me she'd reached Matthew's wife, who had invited her to stay with them. The minute Matthew got home, his wife said, she'd send him over to get Marie.

Marie had also phoned our neighbor Paul and asked him to come over while we waited. Paul arrived and wanted to know, "Where's Carl's gun?"

Marie ran back into her house and came out, her face ashen. The gun was gone.

"Let's go to your place, Amanda," Paul decided. "We'll wait inside for Matthew."

Saint barked his friendly greeting as I unlocked the door and entered the dark house. To ease our minds I went into each of the three rooms, Marie following close behind, and switched on all the lights.

It was from the bedroom window that I saw them . . .

"Look!" I whispered to Marie.

Standing shoulder to shoulder around the house, just outside the fence, were scores of magnificent glowing figures. Twenty feet tall or more, they were luminescent against the darkening sky, as if their bodies were made of light. They stood with their backs to us, facing outward; each one carried a shield and a long spear at his side. Strangely, I felt no surprise at seeing them. It seemed right and natural that they should be there.

"Look at what?" Marie asked.

"Those men . . . angels . . . whatever they are. Marie, there must be a hundred of them!"

Marie stepped to the window and peered out. "Are you feeling all right, honey?" she asked. "There's nobody out there." She took me by the arm and drew me out to the kitchen. "Amanda thinks she sees angels in the yard," she told Paul.

Paul looked out the kitchen window, then at me. "Yeah," he said. "There are only two chairs in here," he went on, clearly happy to change the subject. He went and got the rocker from the living room.

It was completely dark outside now. Nine o'clock came, and no Matthew. Then, about 9:15, Saint gave his Matthew bark.

"He's here," I said, jumping up to grab Saint by the collar. "Hush, Saint!" But the dog kept up his low, ominous growl.

I started for the door but Paul stopped me. "Don't open it till you know who's there!" he warned. I went to the window. I could see the shining beings keeping guard around my fence, but no one else. Finally I let Saint go.

"What was that all about?" Paul asked.

"I don't know. There's no one out there but . . ." "Your angels?" said Paul.

Another forty-five minutes passed. Ten o'clock. I made a second pot of coffee. "Why don't I take you to Matt's place, Marie?" Paul asked, but Marie was sure Matthew was on his way.

Then, a second time, the hair on Saint's neck bristled and he began his Matthew bark. We waited for our big friend's voice or knock, but once again we heard nothing. At 10:45 Saint repeated his performance. "You say Saint barks like that only for Matthew—well, where is the guy?" Paul wanted to know. "I'll bet it's Carl out there."

"Saint never barks at Carl," I said.

At 11:30 Marie gave in and agreed to go to Paul's house, where there was a sofa bed in the living room. They asked me to come too, but I wanted to stay in case Matthew finally showed up. Paul looked out the window. "Are they still here?"

"Yes," I said, "and I've never felt safer."

Paul and Marie left. I washed the coffee cups, put the rocker back in the living room and got into bed. As I closed my eyes I thanked God for sending His angels to protect us. Then I turned out the light and immediately fell asleep.

Next morning I ran from window to window to see if the luminous beings were still there. I counted only four of them now, one at each corner of the fence. *Guess we don't need a whole army now,* I thought.

Paul phoned; I told him that Carl hadn't returned. A few minutes later Paul drove Marie over. "How are your angels this morning?" he asked with a smile. I told him four were still here, keeping watch. "Sure," he said.

Around ten o'clock Saint began growling—that unmistakable Matthew bark. And this time, through the kitchen window, I saw our friend on the front steps. I put the dog in the bedroom and all three of us went to the door to greet him.

"Where were you last night?" Paul demanded.

"Where was I?" Matthew asked. "Where were you? That's the question."

"Right here," said Paul.

Matthew laughed. "No, you weren't. I came by three times and there was no one here . . . except that dog, raising a ruckus."

Paul sat down hard on the sofa. His jaw dropped as Matthew described how he'd come by at roughly forty-five-minute intervals the night before. "Your cars were here. That's what was so strange," he said. "Saint would have eaten me up if I'd tried coming inside, but I walked around and looked in all the windows. The rocking chair was in the kitchen," he added with a puzzled frown. "The place was empty, I tell you. If you were here," he said, "you were invisible."

I stared at him. "Then you had to be invisible too, Matthew," I said. "We didn't see you or hear you."

"But if Carl was out there somewhere—" Marie began.

"And if we'd opened the door to let Matthew in . . ." said Paul.

The four of us sat blinking in the bright May morning. What mysterious protection had hovered over this house? It was Paul who told Matthew about the angels circling the fence.

There was much we didn't understand—have never understood, and maybe are not meant to understand. We'll never know what danger waited out there in the dark. Carl says his mind was so fogged by drugs and alcohol that he has no memory of that night.

But whatever the evil, it could not find us; scores of shining beings had made us invisible.

No Such Animal

by Carter Allen

My girlfriend, Dawn, and I stayed out late into the night not long after New Year's Day. It was snowing heavily when we got into my car, and we decided to go only as far as my mother's house, about ten miles away. I drove slowly, the headlights of my compact boring white tunnels in the swirling flakes.

Around 1:30 A.M., about a half hour after setting out, we turned onto Mom's road in a rural area near the northern Minnesota town of Walker. There were only a couple of dwellings on the two-mile stretch leading to her house, and Mom knew all the comings and goings in this quiet area.

By then the storm had become a raging blizzard. The windshield wipers groaned, protesting the mounting accumulation. Ghostly drifts shrouded the road and I tried to keep the wheel steady. I shifted into low gear and Dawn gasped. "Don't worry," I assured her. "We'll make it."

No sooner had I spoken when we hit a hidden dip. The car lurched sideways, and I struggled to regain control as we shot into a ditch. "Hold on," I said. The wheels spun in a futile whine when I pressed the accelerator. We were stuck.

"What now?" Dawn whispered.

"We'll have to shovel our way out as best we can," I said.

I reached onto the floor of the backseat. All I had was a snow-brush. Dawn and I got out. Squinting against the stinging crystals, she wielded the brush and I scooped the white powder with my hands, trying desperately to free up space around the tires. But as fast as we dug, the driving snow relentlessly filled in the gaps.

We looked at each other in desperation. The windchill must have been way below zero, with the gale shrieking off the flat fields bordering the road. Our tennis shoes, jeans, sweaters and jackets were no match for the cold. We climbed back into the car and started the engine to warm up. But in about fifteen minutes it died.

"Snow blocking the exhaust," I sighed. We sat quietly for a

moment, the howling wind stealing through every possible crack. Thick frost built up on the windows.

Think, I told myself. Mom's house was still a good two miles away, too far to walk in this terrible storm.

"Remember that house about a half mile back?" I asked Dawn. She nodded. "Maybe we can get help there."

"I can't think of any other way out," she said. "Let's go. It's worth a try."

Again we ventured into the blizzard, which had now become a whiteout, and plodded through knee-deep drifts toward the house. After some ten yards, I looked back. I couldn't see Dawn. I couldn't see more than five feet.

"Dawn!" I called. "Can you hear me?" Retracing my path, I found her. She looked dazed.

"Thought I was right behind you," she said. She wasn't going to make it. I led her back to the car, settled her in, and took off running as fast as I could to the house.

Finally I stomped onto the dark stoop and pounded on the door. After a while a porch light blinked on and a man pulled open the inner door. I saw him pull the screen door shut.

"I'm sorry to wake you," I said, "but my car is stuck in a ditch, and my girlfriend and I are stranded."

"Can't help you," the man said, his face set. He started to push the door closed. I could see that he was old and afraid to let a young, strange man into his house, but I tried again. "Please, I just need to use your phone."

"Don't have one," he said. "And my car doesn't work. Like I said, I can't help you." He shut the door. The light went off.

What are we going to do? Tears froze on my face as I headed back to the car. My shoulders and back tense from bracing against the driving snow, I trudged on, feeling weaker with every step. Stumbling along, I was dimly aware of something following me. But I was so exhausted, so agonizingly cold, it was all I could do to put one foot in front of the other. I didn't have the strength even to turn around and investigate. Too much effort, I thought sluggishly. "God," I said, "only You can help us now." Then, my head swimming in blackness, I pitched forward into a drift . . .

When I came to, a prickly, hairy form covered me like a blanket. *What . . . ?* Some sort of a huge black dog was lying on top of me. "Good boy," I whispered, rubbing my hands in the stiff fur under his neck. *Is he wild?* I wondered. No pet would be out in this weather. I looked into his eyes. He seemed somehow to want to help me, almost as if he knew why we had crossed paths.

I pressed my face into his thick fur and breathed the air warmed by his body. The dog stood up.

What a magnificent animal, I thought. I had never seen a similar breed. Feeling new strength, I rose and headed for the car. I half expected the dog to continue on with me, but looking back I saw nothing; my dark rescuer had disappeared into the storm.

I found Dawn shivering. "I didn't have any luck at the house," I told her. "But on the way back, something incredible happened."

We huddled close in the backseat, and I began to describe my encounter with the mysterious black dog. "What was he like?" Dawn asked. "Was he beautiful?"

I stretched out the details, making the story last. Just the telling of it warmed me, and I could feel Dawn relax in my arms.

When morning light brightened our snow-covered windows, we heard the roar of a snowplow. Then someone rapped on the glass. The Good Samaritan driver took us to my mother's house. "You were out all night in that awful storm?" Mom said. "God must have been watching over you."

I told her about the black dog who saved my life, and she looked doubtful. "I know my road," she said. "There's no such dog around here."

Then her eyes widened. "But, you know, twice I've seen a black wolf wandering around that very spot." She stopped. She knew it as well as I did. That dog, or wolf, or whatever it was, wasn't wandering. It had been sent.

ANGELS IN THE

ARD

In the aftermath of the Oklahoma City bombing, which drastically changed their lives, where did Connie and Art Smith find the messengers who prompted them to take a new look at their faith and their marriage? In their very own yard. And Elizabeth Purdy was amazed at the sight outside her window on a September afternoon.

Go ahead. Sometime in the next day, look up and look out. See what delight God has for you right outside your door.

When the Grass Stopped Growing

by Connie Lynne Smith

On what was surely the hottest day of June, I stood waiting in our front yard. I looked down the road for the pickup that was supposed to deliver new topsoil. The driver had called at noon, asking for directions to our house in suburban Kansas City. Half an hour later he called again. My husband, Art, said, "Stay right where you are and I'll come get you."

For more than a year everything had gone wrong. Our troubles began on April 19, 1995, when the Alfred P. Murrah Federal Building in Oklahoma City was bombed. Among the victims was Art's younger brother, Mike. Mike had three children, all teenagers, who had already lost their mom the year before.

After the funeral Art was appointed their legal guardian. Mike's daughter was seventeen, and she wanted to stay with friends in

Oklahoma City; the two younger boys came to Kansas City to live with us. The next nine months passed in a blur of visits to doctors, therapists, lawyers and juvenile authorities. We did everything we could to help the boys. Finally, counselors convinced us they would be better off back in Oklahoma City with friends, where special programs had been set up for kids who had lost their parents in the bombing.

Art and I had been stretched to the limit. He had missed a lot of work taking trips to Oklahoma City, and we were deep in debt. Art had been so busy serving as Mike's children's guardian that he hadn't had a chance to mourn his brother's death properly. I came down with a serious ear infection. I had always thought our marriage was rock solid, but under the strain of the previous year we were at loggerheads. For the first time in our lives, Art and I were unable to do much good for each other.

Then the grass in our front yard died—certainly not a catastrophe, but for us it was the final blow. We watered it. We seeded it. We spread fertilizer. The only choice remaining was to lay new sod. First we had to bring in a load of soil to fill in the low spots, though. *Dear Lord,* I prayed that day as I waited for the delivery to arrive, *let this be a new start for Art and me too.*

Finally Art rounded the corner, followed by the rattling and shaking truck carrying the load of topsoil. As the pickup came to a stop, out stepped a cheerful-looking man. "I'm Corky," he said, flashing me a grin. He wiped the sweat from his face with his handkerchief, then introduced me to his wife, Trudy, and their cherubic son, James, who'd tagged along. Then we four adults began unloading the dirt.

Even on that sweltering day Corky had a way of making the work seem light. At one point he leaned on his shovel and gestured to the statue of Mary we had in the garden. "You folks must be Christians," he said. When I nodded he said, "So are we. Protestants." All at once it struck me that Art and I had not been steadfast in maintaining our daily commitment to our faith, almost as if we had let our troubles slip ahead of our relationship with God.

When our sweaty work was done, I invited everyone to the front porch for iced tea and lemonade. Trudy told us how they'd recently moved to Kansas City from Atlanta and were just settling in. They'd endured many struggles along the way, but their faith had given them strength. We told them about our sorrows. "Trust God," Corky said. "He'll pull you through." He glanced at Art, then at me. "Looks like the two of you have always been able to rely on each other too."

I reached over and patted Art's hand. He smiled. "Yes, sir, we have," he said. In that instant the closeness we'd shared for nineteen years came back full force.

I didn't want our time together on the front porch to end. In Corky and his family's presence our worries seemed to fade. "Please, stay for dinner," I said.

"Thanks, but I'm afraid we can't," Corky answered. "We have to get the truck back."

Trudy stood. "Keep the faith," she whispered as we hugged good-bye. I watched the ramshackle truck drive off and disappear around the corner. Art and I admitted we felt as if a huge weight had been lifted from us. "Angels couldn't have done us any better," Art said.

Beginning with that visit our marriage was revived, our faith strengthened. We have been reimbursed for many of our debts by disaster-relief programs. Art's nephews continue to work through their grief, and Art has finally had time to mourn his brother's death. We know people all over America prayed for us. And if you're wondering about the lawn, it's as green as a golf course. There was something very special indeed about that load of topsoil!

Angels for Amber

by Elizabeth D. Purdy

The rough mile-long path to the front door of our new home meandered over the hills, creeks and cattle guards of a neglected country estate. Vegetation threatened to engulf the abandoned mansion along the way. The run-down condition of the fourteen-hundred-acre spread had been a big reason we'd been able to rent the estate manager's old house for a pittance. I loved the peaceful isolation of the countryside. Our three little ones—a newborn, an eighteen-month-old and a three-year-old—were too young to be affected by our move, but I worried that it might be a difficult transition for Amber, who would start at a new school in the fall.

Even with the bargain rent, we struggled to get by. My husband took construction and drywall jobs wherever he could get them, working sixty-hour weeks, often nights and weekends. The children required at least the same amount of time from me, and I appreciated Amber's eagerness to help. She loved to be a little mommy. Her independent spirit made it easy to let her look after herself. Still, I worried. She was, after all, only six. Someone had to look out for her too.

When it was time to sign Amber up for kindergarten, she was excited. I couldn't help thinking, though, that, with her spending all day in a classroom, I'd be there for her even less.

On the first day of school Amber trotted downstairs in her new red-plaid skirt, white blouse and kneesocks. Her wispy brown hair curled around her face, setting off her big dark eyes. She had gotten ready all by herself and waited patiently while I settled the three little ones into the car.

In the mornings I could drive her down the rugged trail to our mailbox and wait for the school bus with her. But in the afternoons the babies would be napping, and I couldn't leave them. Amber understood that when the bus dropped her off she would have to make the mile-long walk home alone. "Hon, I'll be waiting on the front porch when you get here," I assured her with a kiss and a squeeze as the school bus approached. She hopped on, waved and was gone.

Throughout the day I pictured Amber sitting at a small desk, coloring, reciting the alphabet and playing with new friends. *She'll be fine,* I told myself. But as I stepped out onto the porch that afternoon, I realized with a start that the red speck streaking across the far hilltop must be Amber. Her little legs pumping, she tore through the overgrown weeds along the path. As she got closer I could hear her hysterical cries. Her eyes were wide with terror.

"Sweetie, I'm right here," I said, darting across the yard.

"Mawwwwmy!" she wailed, flinging herself into my arms. "I can't walk home all by myself!" she choked. "I can't!" I hugged her until she caught her breath, then smoothed her hair. Her face was streaked with tears, and one sock sagged around her ankle.

That night when I read from the Bible to the children, I made a point to choose verses about courage and protection. Then I said good night to the babies and sat on the edge of Amber's bed. "I know it can be scary to walk home all by yourself," I said, tucking the blankets around her. "But God is looking out for you, and so am I." She nodded and I kissed her forehead before turning out the light.

The next morning as we drove down to the bus stop, I told her, "Remember, I'll be waiting on the porch for you." I hoped Amber's journey would be less frightening for her, having done it once already. Around three o'clock I pushed open the screen door. Minutes later Amber tumbled into the yard, in tears again. Each day thereafter was no better. I felt guilty standing on the porch, straining my eyes to see her sprinting over the hill half a mile from home. There had to be a way to make this easier for both of us.

My husband and I decided to take a family outing down the lane that weekend. We dressed the kids in jackets and boots and spent most of an afternoon going up the drive to the mailbox, where the bus dropped Amber off, and back down again to the front yard. Along the way we picked up leaves drenched in the rich hues of autumn and pointed out that the most beautiful ones had fallen from the tallest trees. We tottered over the bars of the cattle guards, showing Amber how to keep her balance and walk sideways across them so her toes wouldn't slip through. We named the cows and sang songs. We even caught a butterfly. I held it carefully in the palm of my hand as Amber looked in amazement.

We toured the dilapidated old mansion, investigated the woods, splashed across streams, and scrambled right up the biggest hill of all. I'd never realized how rugged the path could be on foot!

All day long Amber toughed it out with us, most of the time as our fearless little leader. If only her security would last when we couldn't be with her.

Amber made it to the porch without sobbing on Monday, but within a couple days her fears of snakes in the water and creatures in the woods had returned. "There are ghosts in the mansion," she complained. "And the trees are big and mean." What else could I do?

Then one night I was reading aloud from the Old Testament when Amber asked what angels were. I hadn't thought about angels in a long while and took a moment before answering. "God uses angels to protect us from harm," I said. "He calls upon them to watch over us."

Her eyes bright, she exclaimed, "Let's pray for angels to be with me when I walk home from school!" So we did. Amber prayed for her angels, and I prayed that God would not let her down.

The next afternoon I put the little ones in bed for their naps and went to stand watch on the porch. *Lord, we're counting on You,* I prayed. *Please, send angels for Amber.* I waited, a knot in my stomach.

As soon as I saw her crest the hill, I noticed something odd. Amber was not running. She wasn't even in a hurry. What had gotten into her? From my vantage point she seemed to be skipping or even *dancing* across the grassy hilltops. And something was moving along with her. Butterflies! Hundreds, perhaps thousands, arced above her in a satiny canopy.

Amber stopped to twirl under them before they floated to the ground like a carpet laid out before her. She seemed to be laughing as she tiptoed to the edge.

Instantly the butterflies rose up and over her as one wide swath and took a gentle lead. They fluttered farther up the hill, then glided down again. Amber scampered up to meet them, and they hovered over her as before, then drifted ahead.

Repeating this spectacular pattern up and down the hillside, through the woods and over streams, the delicate flight escorted

Amber right to her own front yard, where as one they rose for the last time and flew high over the mountain behind our house.

"Did you see them, Mommy?" Amber asked, jumping up and down. "Did you see my angels? When I got off the bus they were by the mailbox, waiting for me." I hugged Amber to me. "I'm never going to be afraid to walk home again."

I love to think of nature as an unlimited broadcasting system through which God speaks to us every hour, if we will only tune in.

~ George Washington Carver

ANGELS AT

ZERO HOUR

The military uses the term zero hour *to describe the very moment of action. Here, at the end of our everywhere alphabet, we see evidence of God's power to avert disaster just in the nick of time. The last story, "Coming Clean," is a special reminder that God's messengers come in many disguises. You never know who that angel of mercy might be.*

No Human Voice

by Robert J. Keirn

I was a fitter working the afternoon shift at Pennsylvania Engineering in New Castle, Pennsylvania. We were making blast furnaces for steel mills to burn out impurities from iron ore.

Like most factories, it was a noisy place with the floor-shaking thump of giant metal-cutting shears, the ear-splitting whine of welding machines, and the constant clanging of men swinging sledgehammers on steel.

After nine years there I had gotten used to the din. My job was constructing the metal cone-shaped top of a furnace. At age sixtyone, I was proud of my work as a class-A fitter; it took skill to assemble those complicated units. When completed they would be mounted on the furnaces, which stood from one to three stories tall. The tops, about twenty-two feet in diameter and nine feet high, were composed of twelve triangular sections welded together to form the rounded conical structure.

Each one-and-a-half-ton triangular section was made of one-and-a-half-inch-thick heavy-gauge steel, six feet wide at the base and nine feet high. These would also be welded to the base of the cone, a giant steel ring about two feet high. Amid the odor of steel dust, I stood inside the ring to fit the sections. One by one they were tack-welded into place.

I was working with a helper on the first section when the trouble happened. The section was supported from above by a big crane. Propping it up from below was a heavy-steel angle iron extending from the floor to the upper part of the section. Using a turnbuckle arrangement, I was starting to fit the huge triangular section onto the ring when the supervisor came over. "Bob!" he yelled above the roar to get my attention. "The welding department needs the crane. We're going to move it."

I looked at him, puzzled. Without the crane, the section would be supported only by the angle iron. There was nothing I could do; the work had to go on.

Straddling the angle iron, I carefully began to edge the section into place. The scream of a nearby welding machine pierced my ears, but I concentrated on making the fit. It had only an inch to go when I heard a strong voice shout with powerful authority, "Bob, move!"

No human voice had spoken. Except for my helper on the other side of the section, there was no one else around. Yet, instinctively, I leapt from the angle iron to the side. At that exact instant, the one-and-a-half-ton steel section crashed down. It glanced off my shoulder, knocking me to the floor. If I had been straddling that angle iron, I would have been cut in two. As it was, I suffered a double-compound leg fracture and a severely dislocated ankle.

After a week in the hospital and a long recuperation, I was well enough to walk with crutches. Though I haven't been able to work since then and still limp, I am grateful to the Lord for saving my life.

The way I see it, God is everywhere. And if we're tuned in to Him, we'll hear Him, just as I heard His angel shout at that critical moment, over all the clamor.

Coming Clean

by Marie Taft Turley

The summer after I turned sixteen, I bused tables at a cafeteria on the Army base where my father was stationed. The regulars, a lively mix of soldiers and civilians, said they could tell by the gleam of the chrome when I was on the clock.

I walked through the dining room with my brown uniform freshly laundered, apron starched, shoes polished, a colonel's daughter to the core. I joked with customers above the clattering coffee cups and jukebox tunes and cleaned the Formica tabletops with four deft turns of my rag. Every aspect of my first job was orderly and perfect, except one. And I was expecting him any minute.

At exactly 10:45 A.M. my nemesis darkened the door. He was punctual and consistent—his only redeeming qualities. I sighed as the bum slouched into the immaculate booth to wait for his scruffy buddies. My handiwork would be wrecked before the lunch-hour rush. He was unkempt, inconsiderate. I had the feeling he'd never held an honest job a day in his life.

As customers poured in, I concentrated on my station. It was hard to ignore the swear words and cigarette smoke billowing from Table 32. *Keep your voices down,* I silently scolded, walking briskly by them. *Don't you care that everyone is staring at you?*

Of the three men, the good-for-nothing with shabby clothes and long hair clumped in limp, greasy strands was the worst. He slouched alone on one side of the booth, carelessly spitting tobacco; even his friends kept a safe distance. *Why can't you learn some manners like the rest of the civilized world?*

When they finally cleared out, I confronted the disaster area. *God, I know You must love him, but he makes my job really tough.* My stomach churned as I wiped down the table and seat cushions and replaced damp, splattered packets of sweetener. After a final swipe of the rag I went to the kitchen and stuck my hands under the high-pressure hot-water spray of the dish sink. I thought of my favorite Bible verse as I soaped up a second time: "Create in me a

clean heart, O God; and renew a right spirit within me" (Psalm 51:10, KJV).

At the end of my shift, I stepped out of the cafeteria to breathe fresh air and enjoy the long walk home. But no matter how many deep breaths I took, I couldn't shake the horrible stench of that booth. Ambling down the street, I had a creeping suspicion, and I paused to glance over my shoulder. There was the bum, within arm's reach.

I picked up my pace, but we were headed in the same direction. I was forced to stop at the corner traffic light and could almost feel his breath on my neck.

The smell was overwhelming. *I'm off duty now. Can't you see I don't want anything to do with you?* With a show of exasperation, I huffed to the far side of an older woman and her dog. *He's probably dangerous as well as dirty.* The bum took a long stride and moved behind me.

The second the green light flashed, I glanced both ways and took off into the street. At that very moment, his strong hand on my shoulder yanked me back. *Hey, let go of me . . .* My heart jumped as a white sedan careened around the corner. One step more would have been my last.

With shame and gratitude I shook his hand. For the first time I forgot his appearance and looked into his eyes instead.

"You saved my life. Thank you," I said. He smiled before turning away. I stood on the corner and watched him meander down the other side of the street.

The next day I waited impatiently for 10:45. When the tobacco pouch hit Table 32, my resentment didn't rise. The stubborn spots of judgment had been washed from my heart. Tidying up after this customer was easier now that he'd helped me clean up my act. I no longer called him bum. I called him friend.

A NOTE FROM THE EDITORS

This original Guideposts Book was created by the Book and Inspirational Media Division of the company that publishes *Guideposts,* a monthly magazine filled with true stories of hope and inspiration.

Guideposts is available by subscription. All you have to do is write to Guideposts, 39 Seminary Hill Road, Carmel, New York 10512. When you subscribe, each month you can count on receiving exciting new evidence of God's presence, His guidance and His limitless love for all of us.

Guideposts Books are available on the World Wide Web at www.guidepostsbooks.com. Follow our popular book of devotionals, *Daily Guideposts,* and read excerpts from some of our best-selling books. You can also send prayer requests to our Monday morning Prayer Fellowship and read stories from recent issues of our magazines, *Guideposts, Angels on Earth,* and *Guideposts for Teens.*